# God, Cornbread and Elvis

To Becky & Mike
In Christ
Joe E Pennell

# God, Cornbread and Elvis

**COMMON THREAD MEDIA**

Helping faith flourish.

Library of Congress Cataloging-in-Publication Data

Pennel, Joe E.
   God, cornbread, and Elvis: pondering the things of everyday life / Joe E. Pennel.
     p. cm.
   ISBN 978-1-934314-38-8 (alk. paper)
   1. Christianity--Meditations. I. Title.
   BR123.P46 2008
   242--dc22
                         2008011865


Common Thread Media
101 Forrest Crossing Blvd., Ste. 100
Franklin, Tennessee 37064

Publisher: Dr. Douglas N. Norfleet
Production Editor: Kenneth L. Chumbley
Cover Design: Marc Pewitt

Printed in the United States of America

10 9 8 7 6 5 4 3 2 1

978-1-93431-434-0

Visit the Common Thread Media Web site at www.commonthreadmedia.com

IN MEMORY OF
Mary Ann Haney
servant of the servants of God
my administrative secretary and helper
for twenty-five years

# Table of Contents

Light and Warmth
Good to Be Wrong
Love, Not Perfection
Re-creation
Surrender Is Not a Dirty Word
The Devil of the Noonday Sun

Consumer or Steward?
Free to Give
Serving and Keeping
Something for Which God Does Not Care
The Tall One and the Short One

Offering Ourselves
A World Shorn of God
Getting Our Bearings
The Bodily Glorification of God
What It Is!

# Introduction

In 1977 I started writing a few paragraphs for our weekly church newsletter. I made every effort to set aside time every Monday morning for this purpose. During the week I would try to take notice of life as it unfolded around me. When some person or situation would catch my attention, I would make a note on whatever piece of scratch paper I could find. These notes would inform my Monday morning routine.

One day Elizabeth Duncan, a member of my congregation said, "Joe, this week's article is worth pondering." I made a mental note of her comment and the very next week I called the article "Ponderings." It stuck. So, from that time until now, I am yet to use another caption. Thank you, Elizabeth.

At the urging of my wife, Janene, and my friend and colleague, Dr. Douglas N. Norfleet, I decided to select a few of these Ponderings for this book. As you read them, you will see that many of them are dated. I have made no effort to update them because I did not want to take them out of their context.

In writing these pieces, I have tried to connect to the reader by doing two basic things. First, I wanted to reflect on life from the vantage point of the Christian faith. Second, I have hoped to help the reader to ponder, in a much deeper way, on the meaning of everyday matters.

Not all of these themes have been received with affirmation. People have disagreed and they have said so. From time to time, this lack of concurrence has opened the door for honest non-judgmental discussion. This has taught me that in all opposition, there is some grain of truth that I need to hear. That is what happens when we speak the truth in love.

Finally, I am also grateful for the moving of God's spirit through the lives of people, which has helped me to think about that which is worth pondering and that which is not.

# Advent
# and Christmas

# An Innkeeper Named Joseph

Those of us who do public speaking know that the time will come when we will inadvertently misplace a name or a place. Sometimes we catch ourselves, and at other times we are not able to see what we have done. More often than not this embarrassing situation will occur at pivotal moments and big events. It will happen after the speaker has written and rewritten, polished and shined, and verbalized until blue in the face. Unless one reads a manuscript, it will slip up on the speechmaker unawares.

It happened to me at the 4:00 PM. Christmas Eve service. The sanctuary was filled to overflowing. Those who could not get into the sanctuary were watching on a large screen in another room. Every detail of the service had been carefully planned. Music, candles, poinsettias, liturgy, and Holy Communion had been put in place to enable the worshipper to experience anew the birth of Christ. No detail had been overlooked. Everything was as planned until the concluding illustration of the Christmas Eve sermon.

As part of my sermon on "Peace," I had a story about the innkeeper. Without knowing it, I used the name of Joseph instead of the innkeeper. I sailed right through the sermon, not in the least aware of what I had done.

I did not know what I had done until just prior to the 8:00 PM service when two dear friends came to me and said, "Do you realize that you used Joseph instead of the innkeeper at the first sermon?"

Though I tried to shrug it off, I was very disappointed in myself. Christmas Eve, of all times! Joseph, of all people! Me, of all people! Suffice it to say that I was far more careful at the 8:00 PM and 11:00 PM services. At those services the innkeeper got the spotlight.

Now that I look back on that embarrassing mistake, three things are worth noting.

First, there were over 800 persons in worship and only two called my attention to my error. Why did not others speak to me? Afraid they might hurt my feelings? Thought everyone else would say something? Perhaps not many knew enough about the Biblical story to recognize the error? Maybe some were not listening, or had drifted off into more typical Christmas Eve thinking? Did not know how to say it? Meant to, but did not? Whatever the reason, no one corrected me, save two.

In the second place, there is a lesson to be learned from the two who dared to offer a kind, yet mild correction. Those two cared enough about me and about the message of Christmas to be helpful. In a word, those two held me accountable and, in so doing, they made for a better sermon at the 8:00 PM and 11:00 PM services.

One of the noticeable failings of this generation is that we do not hold one another accountable. We are timid about offering correction in the spirit of love. I will often let people blunder along, make mistakes, get themselves in trouble, and be an offense to others without saying a loving word. In so doing, I am contributing to the problem. Most of all, I am not doing that which is loving if I do not help others to see how their behavior or mistake is affecting the life and feelings of others. Offering advice and correction in the spirit of Christ can be the highest form of love.

In the third place, making mistakes either in public speaking or in life just proves that we are human. Our Jewish friends offer a prayer at the beginning of the New Year in which they ask God to forgive them of the mistakes that they will make in the year to come.

The God who came in Christ is the God who forgives both what we have done and what we are about to do.

Let's ride a little lighter in the saddle, not be so hard on ourselves, forgive ourselves, and in the spirit of Christian love help others along the way.

It's worth pondering.

# A Christmas Spirit

Heard more than one person say it this year. In fact, I have heard it over and over again. People are saying things like, "I do not have the Christmas spirit this year," or "It just does not seem like Christmas."

It is difficult to know what that kind of statement means. Does it mean that there should be some kind of "feeling" at this time of the year that one does not experience during the other eleven months? Or is there a certain "spirit" that dies on December 26th and does not resurface until who knows when? Is the "Christmas spirit" something that can be created with music, lights, glitter, and special effects? Is it a feeling that was experienced in a time gone by that a person hungers to recapture?

And if there is a Christmas spirit, where is it to be found? In the bustling aisles of a modern-day department store? On a TV Christmas special? While standing in line at the giftwrap counter? While baking favorite goodies for family and friends? Perhaps it can be found while taking Holy Communion, or while lighting a candle on Christmas Eve.

If there is a Christmas spirit, how does one know when it is seen, discovered, or felt? Is there a way to know it like one would know that $2 \times 2 = 4$? Or is it something that has been fabricated by the marketplace in order to make another buck on the birth of Jesus of Nazareth?

Because many people know about the Christmas spirit, but never experience what they think it is or should be, there is often great disappointment when December 25th comes and goes—disappointment because nothing happened and not one thing changed.

Last Saturday I went to a local nursery to purchase a poinsettia for Janene. It was a wonderfully sunbathed, crisp morning. The nursery was tastefully decorated with ribbons, greenery, and oversized bows. Hot cider and cookies were being served to all of the customers. Balled and burlap trees were being offered for Christmas purchase. A delightful fragrance was in the air. A lady was looking for an appropriate wreath for her office door. Candles flickered in the dimly lit room. The adding machine was totaling one sale after the next.

As I approached the salesclerk, I said, "Are things going well?" Without blinking she replied, "Christmas is a horror story; there is no other way to express it; it's just a horror story. And I, for one, will be glad when it is over."

She was obviously experiencing an emotional overload, which she wanted to get beyond as soon as possible. Her harsh words took some of the joy out of my floral gift.

If I am honest, there are times when I have felt like that clerk. Leading a congregation through Advent and Christmas is no easy task. Details are stacked upon details. All that must go into the four Sundays of Advent and the three services on Christmas Eve is enough to create a mild stress, if not sheer panic. Putting it all together is like trying to move heaven and earth.

But in the midst of it all there is something else. Something eternal is in the midst of the chilling commercialism, people spending money they cannot afford on presents we neither need nor want, the plastic tree, the cornball manger, the Hallmark Virgin, and the earth full of toys.

In the midst of it all there is a creche. And it is at the creche that one is met by the Christmas spirit. Yet, for all of our efforts, we have not been able to ruin the true meaning of it all.

It's worth pondering.

# Bottom Lines and Higher Meanings

Christmas decorations went up in a nearby department store on the day after Halloween. Secular Christmas starts early, and it comes to a screeching halt when the stores close on Christmas Eve.

The religious observance of Christ's birth begins later. The Church begins to anticipate Christ's birth on the first Sunday in Advent, and it concludes on Epiphany Sunday with the remembrance of the visit of the Wise Men to the Christ child.

These two Christmases travel side-by-side, but they stand for two different realities.

James M. Wall has observed, "The agenda of secular Christmas involves memories and the joy of receiving gifts. It draws from religious imagery to evoke emotions regarding gift-giving and selflessness, but it never acknowledges a basic contradiction in its approach: *no gift ever delivers what we long for.* What we long for is a connection to the eternal—something no train set or bicycle can provide. We encounter this disappointment as children, but we continue to long for fulfillment when we hear the promises of the season. When it is over, if we have been locked into the mind-set of secular Christmas, we are left with that post-Christmas depression. The feeling is usually blamed on too much food or too great a reliance on credit cards, *but it has much more to do with unfulfilled expectations than it does with unwise indulgence.*"

A religious celebration of Christmas has a different agenda. Christians celebrate nothing less than God's intervention into human history. It affirms the transcendence of God.

The great Russian writer Dostoevski warned that once transcendence disappears, "everything is permitted." If transcendence has disappeared from our consciousness, then we have every reason to do as we please with Christmas.

When a department store begins playing "Silent Night" before Thanksgiving, and when decorations go up the day after Halloween, there is a real danger that we will miss the mystery of it all. There is an alarming danger that the "bottom line" will be put above the "higher meaning."

It's worth pondering.

# Consumption and the Creation of Wealth

My mind argues with itself about consumerism and the creation of wealth. On the one side I see the importance of creating wealth. Were it not for the creation of wealth, there would not be sufficient employment, educational institutions could not be sustained, social agencies would falter, art and music would not flourish, and the institutional church could not survive. I, for one, would not want to deny that many areas of our private and public life are tied to the creation of goods and services.

On the other hand, I am bothered by the dependent consumerism of our day. In 1976 there were 9,000 items on the shelves of supermarkets. Today over 30,000 items weigh down the shelves. In 1993, 3,000 new health and beauty care products were introduced. Last year 1,300 new beverages were put on the market. I am told that the Mall of America near Minneapolis has 40 million visitors annually. And most of the retail profits are generated during the days that precede our Lord's birth.

Consuming, like drugs or work, can become an addiction. When consuming becomes an addiction, we are trying to medicate the void in our lives with more things. However, if the acquisition of things could make us happy, why are there so many miserable people in America? If consumerism is the answer, why are the rates of divorce, suicide, abortion, and substance abuse so high? Does the ability to consume actually bring meaning into our lives?

I have a wealthy friend who says that he feels morally obligated to reflect upon how his income can be used for the uplifting of humanity. He says that those of us who have the resources for consumption need, for the sake of our souls, to be concerned about our legacy. He preaches that we need not stand at the end of our lives, only to look back and see little more than the anxious accumulation of things.

John Wesley, the founder of Methodism, must have been concerned about this very issue because he said that we should "Earn all we can, give all that we can, and save all that we can."

This Holy Season provides us the opportunity to revalue our values in the light of the One who was born in Bethlehem. In the name of the One who came to bring life and to bring it abundantly, I am grateful for those who create wealth and for those who use it for the uplifting of humanity, and I feel sad for those who falsely believe that having, leads to meaning in life.

It is worth pondering.

# God's Grammar of Love

Christmas is a time when we understand that God's way is often more like the whisper than the shout. When something very special is to be spoken, it is often said with a whisper. Upon receiving a significant gift the receiver whispers, "Thank you." After experiencing a magnificent symphony, the audience will whisper its approval, before breaking forth into thunderous applause. Indeed, the most important moments of life are shared with a hushed tone.

When a man first tells a woman of his love for her, he does not shout, "I LOVE YOU!" Instead, he quietly and gently whispers, "I love you." She returns his love, not with clapping or yelling, but with an almost inaudible whisper.

In the stories, meanings, and symbols of life, God often whispers to humankind. From the foretelling of the Old Testament, until the birth of an innocent, vulnerable baby, God whispered God's profound love for people. Advent and Christmastide, more than any other time of the year, are seasons of God's whispering love. In the Word made flesh, God does not holler at us. No! In the birth of God's babbling child in a Bethlehem manger, God speaks gently, softly, and quietly.

Our society, unfortunately, wants to shout about Christmastide. Boisterous parties, banging parades, jangling TV commercials, and ear-bursting music seem unlike the whisper of God's way.

One of the reasons that the Christmas carol "Silent Night" is so universal in its popularity is that it almost whispers about the birth. Sing it loudly and its meaning will be violated. The softer it is sung, the closer one comes to the richness and depth of its meaning.

God has a wonderful way of avoiding redundancy. No snowflake is geometrically the same as any other snowflake; no person's fingerprint matches any other's; no set of genes is assembled in the exact order of any other arrangement of genes. God, likewise, comes in many ways. But no way is more powerful than the whisper of an innocent baby.

The whisper, not the shout, is God's grammar of love for most of life.

It's worth pondering.

# How to Wait and Where to Look

As a child I remember that the most difficult part of Christmas was simply waiting for it to arrive. From Thanksgiving to December 25th seemed more like an eternity than a month. Days seemed like weeks. Weeks felt like seasons. Time seemed to stand still.

Waiting is foreign to those of us who are accustomed to moving in the fast lane. Waiting seems unnatural. Knowing how to wait is, at best, an uncommon trait. We hunger for immediate satisfaction. The idea of delayed gratification is a stranger to our thinking.

Our society is alive with the symbols of our unwillingness or inability to wait. Exquisite taste does not sell TV dinners. Not having to prepare a meat-and-two-vegetable dinner is what makes this fare popular. Prepackaged vegetables in sealed bags are popular, because they can easily be dropped in a 1½ quart pan of boiling water. Fast-food chains are booming because we can move through a little crooked line, call out an order, sit down, eat, and rush on to the next lap of the rat race.

Condensed books are popular with busy people who do not have the patience to work through interesting sentence structure, innuendo, and the implications and subtleties of a great work. Time must be saved for greater responsibilities!

People no longer want to dine. The leisurely meal, good conversation, and soft music are sacrificed for fast service, the check, the tip—and all because of busy schedules.

Waiting is difficult for modern people. We become ill, and we want to be made well now, not later. Medications, physicians, pastoral care, and love are often rejected if they are not swift. We want a miracle drug, the right prescription, and the best surgeon, so that we can suddenly be back to our hurried routines. Six weeks out of seventy-five years is a low percentage of sick time to healthy time, but we must recover immediately because we do not know how to wait.

Waiting is like living in the meantime. It is like knowing but not knowing. It is how one waits that matters.

God's clock is wound a different way. Time is different. Waiting, not hurrying, is one of God's characteristics. Waiting, God often tells the human, is the appropriate posture.

There are two ways to wait during Advent. Some will wait with a hollow stare. Others will wait with anticipation. Knowing how to wait and where to look for Christ's coming is essential for the Advent season. People will look for

Christ in a variety of places at this Advent. Some will look for his presence in the quiet visit of an old friend. Others will look for a sign of God's coming in the reading of scripture, the thrill of a great novel, the majestic rhythm of an ageless poem, or in the sights, sounds, and symbols of congregational worship.

Knowing how to wait and where to look is like the prelude to Messiah's birth. It's worth pondering.

# The Difficulty of Believing Alone

Next to the infant Jesus, Mary is one of the central characters in the stories about the birth of the Messiah. Our image of Mary has been shaped by Christmas cards and pageants that depict her humbly looking into the manger at her newborn child. The Gospel of Luke pictures her as a model of subordinate service, displaying such virtues as patience, gentleness, submissiveness, and attentiveness.

Rarely do we reflect on how Mary felt when she discovered that she had conceived and would bear a son. Luke says that she was perplexed, afraid, and full of questions about how such a thing could be. In her first appearance on the stage of history, she is not the calm, strong, young woman of faith. In the beginning she cannot sing. She can only question in her heart. She is "afraid," says Luke.

Having heard the message that she would be the mother of the One who would be called the Son of God, Mary went to visit her cousin Elizabeth. When Mary came to her cousin's house, Elizabeth confirmed what God was doing in Mary's life. Elizabeth interpreted for Mary, confirmed for Mary, and helped Mary to understand the action of God in her life. Elizabeth said, "Blessed are you among women, and blessed is the fruit of your womb—and blessed is she who believes that there would be a fulfillment of what was spoken by her Lord." It was Elizabeth who helped Mary to see what God was doing in her life.

It is worth noting that Mary sang the "Magnificat" not before, but after Elizabeth had helped her to see and understand what God was doing through her.

As we move closer to the Manger, we need to remember that *alone* we cannot always believe there will be a fulfillment of God's promises. We need to come together like Mary and Elizabeth did. We need our brothers and sisters in the faith to believe that the promise is with us, for us, and through us. At times, we need others to help us understand.

It is worth pondering.

# Joseph

Joseph was in a bind! Mary, his betrothed, had become pregnant. Both law and custom were on his side. Joseph could have broken his vow to become her husband, thereby putting Mary to shame. Or, he could have divorced her quietly, thereby leaving her in an untenable position. He could have charged her with infidelity, thus repudiating her and reducing her to a life of shame.

While Joseph was trying to decide what to do, an angel of the Lord appeared to him in a dream and said, "Joseph, Son of David, do not fear to take Mary for your wife, for that which is conceived in her is of the Holy Spirit. She will bear a son, and you shall call his name Jesus, for he will save his people from their sins."

According to the customs and standards of his day, Joseph had every right to divorce Mary quietly. Law and tradition were his allies. All of Joseph's customers would have understood. Not one person in the village of Nazareth would have argued with him. He could have slipped out of a most difficult situation.

But instead of taking the easy way out of his bind, Joseph heeded what the angel of the Lord commanded and took Mary as his wife. Instead of trying to find some way to separate himself from Mary, Joseph loved her and cared for her. For Joseph, care was more important than conventional expectations. Compassion was more important than honored rights. Love, justice, and a sense of responsibility were more important than tradition and law.

The biblical story of Joseph makes the heart grow soft. This is so because Joseph was true to his understanding of what God expected of him. He did as

God commanded when law, tradition, and custom gave him permission to take a road much wider and much less difficult. Instead of taking the wide path, Joseph cooperated with the action of God in human history.

He did as the angel requested: he named his son Jesus, which is a Greek form of the Hebrew "Joshua" meaning "he shall save." As the ancient saviors of Israel saved their people from foreign oppressors, so Jesus was to save people from sin.

How we at this Advent and Christmas season can be like Joseph is worth pondering.

# Knowing the Time

For our children, Christmas is in the distant future; for adults, Christmas is just over the fence. For youngsters, Christmas is a long journey; for grown-ups, it is just around the corner. When I was a child, I thought December was the longest month of the entire year. I would get a commercial calendar and "X" off the days, hoping that such "Xs" would somehow hasten the coming of Christmas. The closer I got to Christmas, the farther away it seemed. Christmas Eve felt like the longest day of the entire year.

When we become adults, Christmas comes too fast. Time rushes by. There is so much to do in so few days. There are gifts to buy, ceremonies to arrange, families to entertain, courtesies to care for, and protocol to move through. Christmas seems all too immediate and all too soon.

For children and adults the coming of December 25th shapes our lives between the first Sunday in Advent and Christmas Day. It determines how we will live between "now" and "then."

In 1966 I was the associate pastor of St. Luke's United Methodist Church in Memphis, Tennessee. On a spring, Thursday afternoon, the White House called to tell us that the vice president of the United States would be worshiping at St. Luke's Church the following Sunday morning. From Thursday afternoon until 10:50 AM Sunday morning, Mr. Humphrey's expected visit gave shape to our actions as a congregation. His coming determined how we would spend those few brief days. We knew that we must be ready for his arrival.

The earliest Christians earnestly believed that their lives were shaped by the Second Coming of Christ. They were convinced of their need to be ready for Christ's arrival, just as St. Luke's Church knew that it must be ready for the vice president's visit. This conviction was one of the towering marks of the early church.

If we believe that the Son of man is coming, then that belief will determine how we live in the present. But, if we do not believe that the Son of man is coming, we will shape the present like the past. Or, we will shape the present as if nothing is about to happen.

I have a friend whose son is a student in a faraway college. This young freshman had not been home since he left in mid-August, but he was expected to return for Thanksgiving. Prior to his homecoming, the family spent their energy getting ready for his arrival. For days, the family anticipated the coming of their child. Preparations were made. His favorite foods were prepared. His room was spruced up and made ready. Members of the family planned to be home for his visit. The actions of the family had meaning and purpose because their present had been shaped by a future event. Likewise, if we believe in the coming of the Kingdom of God, then the Church will try to live every day in anticipation of that event.

But, as we all know, to prepare for a future event is difficult if we do not know when the event will occur. If we did not know when Christmas would come, then it would be difficult to shape our lives around that expectation. If we did not know when our daughter would be returning home from a long journey, then it would be hard to prepare for her homecoming. This Sunday is the first Sunday in Advent, the beginning of the Christian year. The sermon will focus on how it is we are to wait for the One who is yet to come.

How one waits for the God who came in Jesus Christ is worth pondering.

# Neither Destroyed nor Fully Understood

Not many voices say anything profound about Christmas. Every now and then a voice will sound off about its being too commercialized. But not much more than that is ever said, and that is not very much. There is, however, some truth to that observation because it is too garish, harsh, and hard.

Commercialization is seen in people spending money they cannot afford, on presents that others neither need nor want. It is seen in plastic trees, cornball crèches, and in Hallmark Virgins. Seen in music that is too loud and incessant. Seen in stores that pull out the Christmas ornaments even before the pumpkin is put away. Seen in decorations that are too big, too brassy, too tawdry, and too much. Seen in many of our children who know more about the legends of Rudolph, the Red-Nosed Reindeer than about the stories of shepherds and wise people. Seen in those who do not remember the One whose birth is honored on December 25th.

Strange as it might seem, no matter how much we commercialize Advent and Christmas, we cannot seem to destroy the mystery of it all. Beneath all of the hype and glitter there is a meaning that cannot be muffled or erased by either strength or weakness.

Though we cannot ruin it, neither can we fully understand the mystery of it all. We can come close to understanding the mystery, but we cannot fully comprehend it. Try as we might, our finite minds cannot grasp the infinite mystery that the God of creation became an innocent child. The mystery of it all defies our grandest imagination. Perhaps that is why this is such a magical time of the year. There happens to be the daily popping out of lights, the wreaths and tinsel, window displays, and music in the air. There are the colors of reds, greens, golds, and purples. Everywhere you look it's like a magicland out there. But, no matter how much we do, we cannot get fully in touch with the mystery of it all. Even the music, Scripture, and liturgy of the Church cannot completely disclose the mystery of the Incarnation.

A realistic newspaper commentator said, "We need Christmas in a deep and lovely way. We need to feel lumpish in the throat." Surely there is more to Christmas than a lump in the throat; more than a warm, sentimental feeling that bathes across our being; more than a warmth that is not experienced at any other time of the year. And yet, there seems to be an instinct here that is our attempt to grasp a tiny part of the mystery.

All that we do at this season is our attempt to reduce the mystery to some kind of concept that we can understand and experience. The reason that we cannot make sense of the mystery is because Christmas is about what God has done to save humankind. Thus, Christmas cannot be destroyed, nor can it be fully understood.

It's worth pondering.

# Not about What We Do

Too much emphasis is put on what "we do" to prepare for Christmas. Putting up decorations. Selecting and buying of gifts. Trimming a tree. Attending parties. Preparing for an open house. Getting schedules arranged with all of the relatives. Responding to the expectations of others. All of these things have their place as we observe the cultural side of the holiday season.

At the theological level, Christmas is not about what we do. It is about what God has done by coming to us in the innocence and vulnerability of a baby. In the infant, God does not overpower. Nor does God force us to believe.

In a few days it will be Christmas Eve. Families will pile in a car for a drive to the church. People will sit huddled elbow-to-elbow. Even the most skeptical college junior will come. The faithful and the unfaithful will sit side-by-side. Some will look with a blank stare. Others will be wide-eyed and wondering at the mystery of it all.

Even the most doubtful will understand that Christmas is a way of talking about what God has done. It is a way of speaking about God as Emmanuel (God with us).

If we focus too much on what we do, instead of what God has done and is doing, we will have the experience and miss the meaning.

It's worth pondering.

# On Not Bashing Commercialism

I t does very little or no good to bash the commercialism of Christmas. I have done my share of that, but it is like an ant trying to move a mountain! It is of no avail because not many people outside of the Church pay much attention to what we are saying to each other. Our voice, no matter how strident, seems to have very little influence on how society orders its life! In a word, our ranting and railing will not cause commercialism to be erased from this season.

Rather than putting effort into decrying commercialism, the Church needs to put its energy into offering that which no other organization has to give. We should offer that which calls attention to the implications of Christ's birth for our personal and social life. We should point to that which God did in Jesus to show divine love for all persons. All that we do in the Church should point to the Incarnation, to God's coming in a particular person, at a particular time, and in a particular place. God would be better served if we put our effort into that which makes the season holy.

I am pleased that this congregation does just that. We try—through worship, fellowship, teaching, and ministry to the poor—to order our congregational life around that which God came to do in Jesus Christ. For that I am most grateful.

The world beyond the Church might not pay much attention to us, but society did not pay much attention to the birth of Jesus either. Nonetheless, it is our task to keep alive the mystery of what God was up to in the birth of Jesus of Nazareth. If we don't do this, who will?

It is worth pondering.

# The Was-ness and the Is-ness of Advent

I have noticed that there is a bunch of *wasness* about this season of the year. Many of us are fond of speaking about the way things were in times gone by. The wasness of places like Nazareth and Bethlehem. The wasness about Mary, Joseph, shepherds, wise men, innkeepers, angelic choirs, and an infant's birth are forever stamped in our memory.

When families get together, we like to do reruns on how a Christmas past was celebrated: a few toys, oranges, dried applies, popcorn beads on the tree, cracked walnuts, the gathering of relatives, and a bountiful feast.

I can remember those pageants of my childhood. Bed sheets for robes. Towels for turbans. Apple crate boards for a manger. Whatever we could find for the building of a set. My memory tells me that I learned to quote the entire chapter of Luke for a recitation at Jackson Avenue United Methodist Church. All of that and much more represents the wasness of this time of the year.

But there is also an *isness* about this season of the year. In spite of all of the glitz, commercialism, and hype, the believer knows that this is Advent, a time for preparing for the observance of Christ's birth. During this time, some will make spiritual preparation; others will not.

God wants to Advent among us. Wants to come near us. Wants to forgive us. Wants to illumine the darkness of our ways. Wants to give love. Wants to make the presence felt. Wants to fill us with peace and joy. But God will not push His presence on us. Will not intrude. Will not overpower us. Will not make us open our hearts for a real Advent.

At this Advent time God will come to those who open themselves. If we are unwilling to grant God access to our darkness, God can do nothing. Whatever is acknowledged, God can take over. What God is not given cannot be taken away. The brokenness that is not presented to God cannot be repaired. If we bring our sins out of the cellar of our lives, God can forgive, thus breaking the power of those sins that so easily possess us. That, in my judgment, is the isness of Advent.

It is worth pondering.

# Revelation Always Leads

The story of the coming of the Wise Men to Bethlehem is a commentary on the reality of divine revelation. In this story, a star leads the astrologers to behold the newborn king. Herod, on the other hand, hears about the birth, but elects to thwart its meaning for the world.

Thus, Matthew gives us two responses to divine revelation. The one response, as seen in the Wise Men, is to pay homage, to worship, and to bring gifts that represent faith. The other reaction, as seen in Herod, is to try to put to death the One who brought God's supreme revelation.

That seems to be the way it is with the appearance of the Holy. Some respond with faith while others reject. And it is often that way in our lives. There are times when we affirm the Christ, and there are moments when we reject. Most of us are a combination of acceptance and rejection, faith and disbelief, trust and fear.

Though our response to revelation is more mixed than true, God continues to lead us even as the star brought Wise Men to Bethlehem's manger.

The question is not, "Will God lead us?" Without a doubt, God will guide us. That is for sure and certain. The real question is, "Will we follow when God leads?"

This year God will come to us in many ways and will offer to take us in new directions. God will appear to us. God will lead us to see the Christ. Some of us will see and turn away because we do not want the love of Christ invading those kingdoms that we have set up for ourselves.

When the Wise Men saw the Christ they returned to their own country by another way. Let us not miss the symbolic "rerouting" that comes from the intervention of the divine revelation in ordinary life. The biblical word about revelation is that when it is real, it always calls us and produces changes in our lives.

We know that we have seen the Christ when we find ourselves living and loving in a different way.

It is worth pondering.

# Belief

# Reconciling Reason and Faith

Presently, there is a gullible, popular piety in the air that places blind, uninformed faith above reason. This is not a new thing. It has existed for hundreds of years. In the twelfth century an intelligent group of people known as the "Scholastics" challenged superstitious piety by asking strong questions that sought to reconcile reason and faith. The Scholastics wanted to free Christian dogma from contradictions that might cause doubt about the validity of the Christian religion. They sought truth by posing questions, and some of their theological questions seemed ridiculous or even blasphemous to those who insisted on an unfounded and unthoughtful faith.

The Scholastics raised the hard question about the relationship of faith and reason, not in order to disprove faith, but because they believed that reason was a friend to the Christian religion.

In this time when so many are wanting blind certainty over a reasoned faith, it is important to remember that we can exalt God and the human mind at the same time. We can arrive at truth by searching both the mind of God, and by exploring whatever data we can find.

When we search the mind of God with all of our mental and spiritual power, and when we chase truth until we find it, we usually wind up with a religion that has both awe and a judicious, believable, down-to-earth quality about it.

Thus, reason and faith are not to be seen as enemies. They are friends of the first rank.

It is worth pondering

# Is Belief Natural?

Human nature has always wanted to believe in something. It is as natural as breathing. Faith is not an affront. It is instinctive. In my experience, people not only want to believe; they do believe . . . in something or someone.

If people do not believe in God, they will believe in success, power, or prestige. And some who do not believe in God choose to have faith in themselves.

When people do not believe in God, they do not cease to have faith. Rather they shift their faith to someone or something else: gadgets, scientism, sentimentalism, progress, free enterprise acquisition, materialism, cults, or whatever. We cannot cease to believe any more than we can cut off breathing.

Last week I shared a lecture platform with a speaker at Southern Methodist University. In one of his speeches he observed that the real religion in America is "winning," or being Number One. If we cannot say that we are Number One, we are considered failures. If we are not a part of the largest and fastest growing, we have probably missed catching the golden ring.

In my judgment there is nothing inherently wrong with being first, but there is something wrong with believing that first is the only place to be. It is sad not to do one's best, but it is not a mortal failure to do all that one can, and still be number two.

I know that I have an odd view of things, but I would like to hear fans of a second-place basketball team hold their fingers in the air and shout, "We are Number Two," "We are Number Two." It is a sad and terrible thing that our cultural religion only values those who finish squarely on top. Shouting "We are number two" would be viewed with great suspicion.

According to biblical theology, it is not where you are in the pecking order that matters. What matters is whether or not love is present. St. Paul said, "If I have all faith so as to move mountains, but have not love, I am nothing." In our natural desire to believe, we often desire to believe in something temporal like winning, instead of something eternal like love.

Because people do not know in what to believe, they will often turn to machines, plans, and platforms whenever a "true leader" comes. And if no good leader appears, they will often follow poor or false leaders if they possess guile or glamor, or if they fit a projected image of how they think life ought to be.

George Buttrick made this clear when he made the following observation about Hitler: "This Hitler knew. He rushed in to fill the vacuum made by our scientific negations. His speeches were ranting nonsense, but they had fervor; and if choice must be made between rationality and fervor, men will choose fervor. His cause was nihilism, but at least he provided pageantry and a vow unto death; and if men must choose between a scientific 'order of life' on the one hand and nihilism plus banners plus a dangerous commitment on the other, they will choose nihilism."

The crucial question is not: "Will we believe?" but in "whom" will we believe? It's worth pondering.

# More than Jesus

There are times, though probably not enough times, when I think solely about Christ. Nothing more and nothing less. Just Christ. *I think about how Christ is too big for us.* When his sandals pushed against the dust of Palestine, he was too big for them. He would not fit into their narrow definition of things. Their petty loyalties, their tight limits, their tunnel vision way of seeing things. He would not stay inside their narrow limits, legalisms, ritualisms, silly conventions, and provincial attitudes. He was too large for them, and he is etched too big for our boxed-in understanding of how things are, or how we think they ought to be.

*This Christ who is too big for us is marked by a special kind of greatness.* There are two kinds of greatness. There is the greatness of a gigantic, charismatic individual. Such was Napoleon. He was as big to humanity as the Grand Canyon is to nature. And there is the kind of greatness that one finds in Michael Faraday, who pioneered the secrets of electricity. He uncovered something in the universe that people had not previously known. With Faraday, greatness was not in the person, but in what the person revealed. Here is the greatness of Jesus. He revealed a universal truth about the nature and purpose of God. The truth had been there all along, but Jesus revealed it and made it clear. When I think of Christ, I think about how he made some things plain about God.

*This Christ who is big and great is also inescapable.* He is in every person, though some have not yet discovered him. When Faraday let loose electricity in the world, its influence could not be escaped. When Copernicus swung open the gateway of a new era in astronomy, though people had never heard of him, all would share the benefits of his work. John Wesley, the founder of Methodism, spoke of prevenient grace. This is the grace of God which is in every human being. It is the grace that precedes one's coming to faith. So, for me, Christ's influence in the world is beyond escape.

Francis Thompson wrote about the inescapable Christ in his poem, "The Hound of Heaven." He went to London as a student. Fell into evil ways. Lost his money. Became a drug addict. Went from bad-to-worse, until he was holding horses' heads at the curbside for a sixpence. Few people were ever lower than Thompson. Yet he came to believe that Christ pursued him even in his defeat. He was, as he said, chased by the Hound of Heaven. We cannot hold Christ back. He presses on to become the Christ of our experience.

Christ. Just Christ. Think about this human picture of what God must be like. Too big. Too pursuing. A revealer. More than the Jesus of history. He is, for me, the Christ of experience.

That, more than any single question, is worth pondering.

# On Not Misusing the Ten Commandments

The Ten Commandments as contained in the Hebrew Bible (not the New Testament, as one Tennessee legislator proclaimed) are intended to be prohibitions against certain kinds of behavior. They let us know what kind of conduct is to be ruled out, not allowable, and not to be entertained at all.

These short, pithy statements are clear and easy to read. However, they are not so easily understood. Their meaning is deep and profound. They beg for interpretation. For example, what constitutes adultery? What does it mean to take God's name in vain? What is a violation of the seventh day? What kinds of acts show dishonor to one's parents? Are there circumstances that permit killing? Who are the other gods that we are tempted to worship?

In my opinion the Ten Commandments need to be studied, thought about, and reflected upon with some seriousness. In a society that has come loose from its moorings, they can provide norms for a type of public morality. They can provide guidelines that are reliable. Anyone who takes them seriously will know that it is madness to violate these requirements. To do so cannot help but to bring harm, because we do not break them—we break against them.

They are so sacred and so crucial to our understanding of freedom and responsibility that we should not trivialize them. Never should we use them to garner favor! Pastors and politicians should, in honor of such rich meaning, refrain from using the Ten Commandments as theatre.

It is worth pondering.

# Our God or gods!

Yigal Amir, the twenty-five-year-old student who was arrested as the assassin of Prime Minister Yitzhak Rabin, told the police, "I acted alone on God's orders, and I have no regrets." Was he speaking about the God who made all that is, or was he speaking about the god that he made?

There are two affirmations about God in the Bible. On the one side there is the theological affirmation that God is and God made us. On the other side is the psychological affirmation that we make gods and serve them. "In the beginning God created the heavens and the earth," so the Bible states, but throughout its course we keep running on another view: "Where are thy gods that thou hast made?" says Jeremiah; or again: "Shall people make gods for themselves?"

Was Yigil Amir serving the God of love, forgiveness, and reconciliation, or was he controlled by the gods that he made—the inward deities of enmity, greed, or vengeance?

Look with me at those elements that constitute a person's real god. A person's god is that central reliance or central devotion to which one gives the highest allegiance. "He restoreth my soul"—one way or another a person sooner or later says that of his or her real god. "Not my will, but thine be done"—one way or another a person says that to his or her real god.

Yigal Amir was not acting on God's orders. He was clearly acting on his god's command!

Why we serve the gods that we have made, rather than the God whose other name is love, is worth pondering.

# Parker's Questions

A very nice six-year-old boy lives next door to us. Now and then he crosses the driveway to talk. Most of the time he is cautious. We are cautious of each other because we are slowly getting to know each other. Though I do not know a great deal about him, I do know that he is full of questions.

"Why are you watering that tree?" "Where are you going to practice golf again?" "Do you know what my friend looks like?" "How tall is your house?" "When are you going to wash your car again?" Those are the questions that Parker puts to me.

I, for one, hope that Parker never ceases to ask questions, because probing leads to answers. As he grows older, I would be pleased if he would learn to ask crucial and important questions.

What we learn about life tends to fit the shape of our questions. If we ask shallow, superficial questions, we will have a view of life that lacks depth. People who come close to understanding the meaning of life are those who raise and pursue the more difficult and hard-to-understand questions.

Likewise, if our questions about God are narrowly based, then the kind of God that we believe in will fit the shape of our questions.

Too many believers treat God as a mascot, hobby, or household god. Many believers see God as a "buddy," or "the man upstairs," or as a "copilot." Such an understanding of God does not arise from reflective, thoughtful questions.

If we believe without question that God is all powerful and truly rules the universe, we are likely to suppress questions about this all-powerful God's allowance of suffering, injustice, and evil. If we are willing to ask harder questions about, for example, the pain of God, then a wider view of God might begin to emerge.

Some would say that such questioning illustrates a lack of faith. But I am suggesting that asking difficult probing questions might be the prelude to a strong and vital faith. I experience many people who seem to want a simple faith based on shallow dogmatic statements. Yet, I also experience many people who are hungry and thirsty for a faith that really works.

One of the reasons that religion is not more vital to us is that the "God" who is revealed to us is as shallow as our questions.

Some times we do not ask those hard questions until we have come to the end of our rope. We ask ultimate questions when we are alone, afraid, and in the dark. Ultimate questions are asked when every road seems to be a dead-end street.

A theologian, Auden, once observed,
"We would rather be ruined than changed.
We would rather die in our dread than
climb the cross of the moment
and see our illusions die."

The new way of believing that has become so popular in our culture wants all answers and no questions.

Why shallow, cultural Christianity has no tolerance or appreciation for ambiguity or contradiction is worth pondering.

# Raymond, Rudolph, and Otie

Groundbreaking! It's been thirty-one years since I participated in a groundbreaking for the building of a new sanctuary. It was my first assignment as a student-pastor. It happened at a church called "Gratitude."

Gratitude was a rural congregation that had about seventy-five members. Most of the members were well beyond sixty-five years of age, and there were very few children and youth. The old building had been standing for almost one hundred years, and it had not been kept in good repair. Paint peeled. Floors sagged. Pews were split. Carpet was torn. The pot-bellied stove was burned through. No water or rest rooms could be found inside the building.

Some thought that the congregation should close and merge with a nearby church. Others thought that we should patch up the dilapidated building. Another group thought that we should build a new church. It was, by every measure, a tough decision.

The "Official Board," as we called it, met again and again, trying to make a decision that would reflect the best interests of all concerned. The decision was made harder because the people loved each other and no one wanted to hurt another person's feelings. In addition, everyone was kin to everyone else, so both blood and emotions were wound up with one another.

I remember the night that the decision was made. After a long and often heated discussion, Rudolph Williams stood up and said, "If Otie Tims will give $500, I'll give $500." There it was. The ball was now in the court of Otie Tims, the oldest man in the church. "Mr. Otie," as we called him, did not stand, but when he started to speak everyone gave ear. "I'll match Rudolph and then some," he said. He spoke further, "Most of us are older, and we will not need a new building for very long. We do not have many children and youth in this congregation, but we must build this church. Someday the city will be moving in this direction, and I want to have a nice building here for those who will someday come."

Others spoke and pledged their support. After a long discussion, Raymond Williams, Rudolph's brother, said, "We've jawed about this for years—let's vote." The vote was close, but the decision to build carried. Some said it could never be done. Others said it could. Some said that the money could be better spent. Some were satisfied with the old building and the old ways.

Those who wanted to make room for others went to work. Went to work with pie sales, bar-b-que suppers, quiltings, ice cream dinners, and car washes. Likewise, believers dug into their savings accounts and set aside a portion of their income for which was yet to be.

Not one of those people who sat in the Board meeting on that hot summer's night in 1959 are still at Gratitude Church. They have all been transported to the Church Eternal.

Last fall I ran into Glenda, who was thirteen years of age when the decision was made. I learned that she and her son are now every-Sunday members of Gratitude Church. I inquired about the congregation. Since 1959 the church has grown in membership, and a small addition has been added to provide Sunday School space and a fellowship hall. In our conversation Glenda made mention of various people who now belong to the church. Except for Nathan, I did not recognize one name.

The night that Rudolph stood up and pledged $500 was a historic moment in the life of that tiny church. Later, I learned that Rudolph Williams did not have $100, much less $500 on the night that he spoke up. The next day he went to the bank and floated a loan, not knowing how he would pay it back.

A mixture of fear and hope filled the air on the day that we broke ground at Gratitude Church. Some cried and some shouted, but all knew that the future was strangely impinging on the present. All of us knew that we were making room for those whose names we would never know. All of us knew that we had to position ourselves to offer Christ to what would someday become a growing community.

At groundbreaking, Otie Tims turned the first spade of dirt. As Otie pushed the shovel into the rich West Tennessee soil, Rudolph smiled as big as he could. In their hearts both men knew that they were giving birth to a future that would someday belong to whoever might pass that way.

It's worth pondering.

# Sheilaism

Have you heard about a woman who named her religion after herself? She calls it her "faith." If everyone in America did this, we would have 220 million American religions, one from each of us.

Her name is Sheila Larson. She is a young nurse who says that she is not a religious fanatic. She proudly calls her religion "Sheilaism."

About herself she says, "I can't remember the last time I went to church. My faith has carried me a long way. It's Sheilaism. Just my own little voice."

In defining "my own Sheilaism," she said:, "It's just trying to love yourself and be gentle with yourself. You know, I guess, take care of each other. I think He would want us to take care of each other." There is nothing more or nothing less to Sheilaism!

Sadly, Sheilaism somehow seems a perfectly natural expression of current American religious life, and what it tells us about the role of religion in the United States today.

Sheilaism is a watered-down view of religion, which calls for no serious commitment to Christ, God's church, or God's people. It is a religion that requires nothing. Has no cross, no sacrifice, no bearing one another's burdens, no reflection on what God requires of us, no giving of time, resources, or income to other persons.

Sheilaism can get along pretty well in the world. But this form of religion will have difficulty when trouble comes, when anxiety seems overwhelming, when others fail us, when the storms of doubt assail, or when the meaning of life is never clearly understood.

In a word, Sheila can be a nice sweet person, but her life will not count for much. No significant difference will be made in the world. In her brand of religion, Christ will not be lifted up.

Religion, at its best, is more than having one's own private faith. At its best, religion grapples with what is best for the community. It reflects upon a larger responsibility for others. It labors for the common good.

For us our faith is both private and public. We believe in a vital piety linked to a social responsibility for others.

John Wesley said that there is no such thing as a solely private religion. For him, all inward religion had to have a public expression.

The writer of 1 John said, "Let us love one another: for love is of God, and he who loves is born of God and knows God."

Why vital faith is more than Sheilaism is worth pondering.

# Suffering

As a United Methodist Pastor I spend a fair amount of time with people who are suffering. All kinds of suffering cross the path of my life. Yesterday is an example of a typical day. I went to Park View Hospital at 6:00 AM to have prayer with a parishioner who was having six bypasses. When I arrived, he had already been taken to surgery, so I attended to the spiritual needs of his wife. When I arrived back at the office, a man whose mother is facing a life threatening illness was standing in the doorway. We talked. Listened. Prayed. In the afternoon I met with a person who is living with the pain that comes from grief. Later in the afternoon I met with a young mother who no longer feels loved by her beloved. For her, the void is deep and the future is uncertain.

While attending a meeting at the church, a man walked up and shared his need for surgery. Two notes were put in my hands.

Another person told me about a marriage that is in deep trouble.

On and on the list goes. Day after day. Responding as the spiritual leader to the suffering of people is not easy, but it is a privilege. It is special to be allowed to share with others their dark nights of the soul. To be with people as they cope, grow, and understand is an opportunity that should be highly valued by every pastor.

However, attending to the suffering is not only a task of the clergy. It is also a responsibility given to all baptized Christians, because laity, as well as clergy, have many opportunities to witness to Christ's presence at the torn places in life. I see the laity being pastors and priests to one another. Hourly, daily, my heart leaps for joy as I see the hands of laypersons on the hurts and hopes of others.

Experiencing suffering in ourselves and in others raises some fundamental questions: Does suffering elevate or alter one's perception of reality? What can one understand about providence when the good suffer? What does suffering mean for our understanding of God?

It's worth pondering.

# The Centerfold

Did you see *The Tennessean* article on November 10, 1992, entitled, "Meet Barbara Moore, Centerfold"? Barbara Moore, in case you did not see it, is *Playboy's* Miss December. She is a young Nashville model, who is determined to make it to the big time. She says that getting naked before twenty photographers, pouring Hershey's chocolate all over her body, posing for video covers, posing for publicity shots, and interpreting for reporters is an excellent career move.

After she was selected for *Playboy,* Barbara said that her mom did not know what to think. Her father, on the other hand, was proud of her. Her best friend said, "She doesn't care if people will one day judge her. She just feels like that's their problem."

Barbara's understanding of the human body is also worth noting. She said, "And I think a big part of being a woman is being feminine and your sensuality is a good part of being a woman and I think you should be proud of it. I don't think that I should be ashamed of showing it at all. A woman's body is made beautiful. I think more beautiful than a man's body. And I mean really, it's true, everybody thinks so."

She is correct about the human body being beautiful. The human body is beautiful because it is God's good gift and it is pleasing in the sight of God.

In my judgment Barbara is wrong in holding to the belief that the human body should be used to glorify Barbara. According to Christian theology, the body should be used to glorify God, not the person. The extremes to which Ms. Moore is willing to go should remind all of us to resist the temptation to make a god of our bodies. Our bodies are to be used to glorify God and in the service of others.

Sexuality can become exploitative. It can be misused to exploit others, or it can be exploited for profit or fame. To use God's good gift for commercialization and exploitation is to both cheapen and degrade the human personality.

Unless she is acting contrary to her beliefs, I am not mad at Barbara. She is, unfortunately, the values of our society reduced to one person. She represents the masses who do not see the human body as a sacred gift. She is a symbol for the multitudes who do not see that the human body is to be used for responsible, committed, and loving forms of expression.

Why some see the body as an object to be used for pleasure and profit, and why others see it as a sacred gift for the glorification of God, is worth pondering.

# The Illusion of Knowledge

Daniel Boorsun has reminded us that Columbus did not know where he was going. When he sailed from the mouth of the Rio Tento on the morning of August 3, 1492, he believed ocean covered only one-seventh of the globe. That was the conclusion of orthodox Christian authorities. He believed the western ocean narrowed, and that Asia extended farther eastward than it does. After all, many of his carefully studied geographies said so.

After four trips to the New World, he died believing he had been exploring the east coast of Asia. But his path of discovery eventually led Europeans to the knowledge that their certainties about geography had been false.

The notable significance of the voyages of discovery was their discovery of ignorance—of ancient people's ignorance of the world. The more people learned about the world, the more they knew how ignorant they were.

In the early 70s, Janene and I made our first trip abroad. We went to Israel, Greece, and Italy. When we got home, people would ask us what we had learned about the Holy Land and other destinations. Though I never did, I wanted to tell my questioners that I learned how very little I knew.

What was true for Columbus and for Janene and me on our first trip abroad is also true in our understanding of God. The more we think we know about God only leads us to know how precious little we actually know. I have been a serious student of Scripture and Christian theology for most of my adult life. I have tried to probe the deepest of the deep. I have attempted to figure out the meaning of life. I have pondered, probed, untangled, and reflected. My questing has led me to know how little I know.

I reason that my finite mind cannot comprehend the infinite. Thus, my finite mind can only know a tiny bit of the infinite.

In recent days I have come to believe that one does not have to know a ton about God in order to be a firm believer. If we want to know what God is like, we can see that in Jesus of Nazareth. That's enough for me. To know that God is love and that where love is there God is, is enough for me. To know that God, through the Holy Spirit, is present with us is enough for me. To know that God is deep within us and far beyond us is enough for me. To get in touch with what God is doing in my life is enough for me. To know that I am known is enough for me.

I find some relief in knowing that I do not have to know all there is to know about God. And yet, the more I know about the Holy Mystery, the more I hunger to know. And the more I hunger, the more I know that I must empty myself before I can be filled.

It's worth pondering.

# Tolerance

I know that people are no longer whipped through the streets of Boston for being Baptists. Nor are Quakers put to death at the burning stake. Methodists are not stoned as was John Wesley. However, there is a rise in religious intolerance.

In the Middle East, religious intolerance is one factor that keeps alive the bitter struggle between the Arabs and Israelis. David Shipler in his book, *Arab and*

*Jew: Wounded Spirits in the Promised Land*, has written, "The moderate ground is eaten away, yielding to pious extremism on either side. Religion becomes a force for evil. It tears at the soul. It coats warfare and terrorism and hatred with a varnished righteousness." All around the world intolerance seems to have a bright future.

Religious intolerance expresses itself as fundamentalism in most every major religion. Fundamentalism is dangerous because it is intolerant of other points of view. It judges other people only by its understanding of what it thinks is true. It has simplistic, pat answers for complex problems. It is risky because it is myopic, narrow, and exclusive.

Intolerant people and groups do not believe that the truth can be trusted to win its own way if given a fair field. Such people believe that truth must be bolstered by artificial enforcements, heresy trails, excommunication, personal discourtesy, defamation, and the practice of exclusion.

Tolerance, on the other hand, does not mean the absence of belief. Nor does it mean that we are not to believe strongly in some things. Nor does it mean that all beliefs hold equal value. Tolerant people are not those to whom all sides look alike. Rather, tolerant people hold certain essential beliefs to be crucial, while being free to search for new truths and new insights. For example, a man who is certain of his relationship to his wife is free from jealousy. So, a person who is certain of the truth can be courteous to rival opinions.

Great believers are those who hold to bedrock beliefs while trusting the truth to find its own level in a sea of intolerance.

As Jesus said, "You shall know the truth and the truth shall set you free."

It's worth pondering.

# Christian Living

# Laughter: The Hand of God Rocking the Cradle of a Troubled World

**M**any people see the church as a rather dull place; a place where folks are somber, lifeless, and everything but joyous. But many things do happen at church. A few are worth mentioning.

At our recently completed Vacation Bible School, a teacher was giving instructions about the world in which Jesus lived. On this particular day she was telling the class about the foods that were eaten in Jesus' day. She said that boys and girls ate figs, cheese, unleavened bread, fish, fruit, and they drank goat's milk. After hearing the menu, one lad popped up and said, "Yuk, poor Jesus." What Jesus ate was a long way from the fast food to which he was accustomed.

One Sunday morning the organist was playing a loud fanfarish piece for the Prelude. It was just after Easter, and the organist was trying to establish the mood of joy that is reflected in the resurrection.

Although it was a glorious presentation, one lad had his hands cupped over his ears. From where I was sitting I had a good angle on the little boy. When the organist had finished, the youngster looked up at his mother and said, "Thank you, God." He was not giving thanks for the Prelude, but for the fact that it was finally over.

Not even Holy Communion escapes those humorous moments. After partaking of the bread and the cup, a little girl asked if she could have "seconds."

The Reverend Donald R. Choate enjoys telling about a bulletin misprint that took place in one of his former pastorates. When he picked up the worship sheet on Sunday morning, he saw these words, "The Lord gives wisdom to the wide." I hope so, because too many of us fall into that category.

While I was the associate at St. Luke's during the mid-'60s, the senior pastor made a terrible—and still talked about—blunder. The sanctuary had recently been adorned with a new tapestry which hung from floor to ceiling directly behind the pulpit and choir loft. It had been given to the congregation by a graying, old dowager, and the senior pastor was very proud of it.

On the first Sunday that it was presented to the church, the senior pastor publicly thanked the generous giver for the lovely gift. In his concluding remarks he said, "As we come here to worship, I want all of us to be inspired by the lovely tapestry which hangs in my rear." The congregation broke out in laughter, and Dr. Fisher, though embarrassed, was big enough to laugh with them. As the years passed, Dr. Fisher enjoyed telling the story on himself, which is the mark of a big person.

Laughter must be of God, because it is good for the soul. Sarah Cannon likes to say that "laughter is the hand of God on a troubled world." It softens the heart and helps us to unclench our fists and, if it comes from the heart, it has a way of creating a greater spirit of reconciliation and openness.

Helen Caswell has written a poem entitled "God Must Like To Laugh." It's in the form of a children's book and it can be checked out of our church library. It goes like this.

> "God made the world—the heavens, too—
> And night and day, and me and you.
> But along with big things like the sun,
> God must have had a lot of fun
> Attending to each small detail;
> The fragile shell upon the snail,
> The flowers fitted to the bee,
> And little bugs too small to see,
> And camels and the kangaroos,
> And things you only see in zoos,
> The penguin and the platypus,
> The monstrous hippopotamus,
> The wondrous webs the spiders spin,
> The way cats purr, the way dogs grin,
> And just because God took a notion,
> We have whales spouting in the ocean,
> We have the llama and the shrew,
> The green bullfrog and the peacock's blue,
> And snakes and bats and all those others
> That only God could love—or mothers.
> How would God think up all those things?
> The different song that each bird sings,

The cockatoo and crocodile—
I think they must have made God smile;
It must have been the way he played.
And when at last they all were made,
From tiny gnat to tall giraffe,
I wish I could have heard God laugh!

If laughter is good for us, and if it is of God, then why do we look so sad when we worship, and especially when we sing hymns like "Joyful, Joyful, We Adore Thee"?

It's worth pondering.

# That Which Cannot Be Framed or Photographed

He has a wonderful and tastefully appointed library. Books line the shelves like each had been specifically ordered for a particular spot. Nothing out of place; everything in order. That's the way it is in his study, located inside floor to ceiling windows so he can look out onto a yard that should be photographed and written up in *Southern Living* or some such magazine.

Plaques and photographs have been gently hung on the paneled walls, reminders of accomplishments and people who have been important. He is photographed with Ronald Reagan, Howard Baker, Gerald Ford, Winfield Dunn, and Douglas Henry. There are three handsome plaques given by the Tennessee School Boards Association "For Excellent Legislative Efforts In Support of Public Education." Memphis State University gave him the "Milestone of Excellence Award," and Millington First United Methodist Church awarded him two plaques—one for being the choir director for fifty years and one for teaching Sunday School for fifty-one years. Most of these are arranged near a photograph of the State Capitol where he served in the General Assembly for twenty-seven years.

As notable as the photographs and plaques are, they do not tell about the most important things, because the more essential things are abstract and intangible. The transcendent part of him—his ethos, his values, his wit, his being radically true to life as he understands it—these cannot be framed or hung.

What is true for him is true for all persons: that which cannot be reduced to a wall hanging is more important than that which can.

A couple of weeks ago when he was coming out of a coma, I said, "Pops, I was in your study this morning, and I looked at all of the wall hangings, and I want to know which one is the most important to you?" Without blinking, Janene's father said, "Never allow yourself to be impressed by your successes."

That spirit cannot be framed or photographed.

How we get to that way of looking at life is worth pondering.

# Standing on the Shoulders of Those Who Have Gone before Us

Not more than two weeks ago Bishop Robert H. Spain stopped by the church to visit with friends and to see the "goings on" with the new building. Before going out to the building site "Bob," as I call him, and I sat in my office and talked about Methodism in general and about Brentwood United Methodist Church in particular.

We discussed the problems and possibilities of United Methodism and about how Brentwood Church has a major responsibility to be a beacon light to the entire denomination. Bob said, "Since leaving Brentwood and becoming a bishop, I see more than ever that Methodism needs a few congregations that set the pace for all of the rest."

Those of us who study, worship, and serve here are prone to forget this larger responsibility. Our experience with the church universal is at the corner of Franklin Road and Williamsburg Road. It is here that we come to hear the Word, receive the Sacraments, and to be empowered to be Christ's people out there where we live and work.

Bob Spain, in his persuasive and insightful way, has reminded me that we, as Brentwood United Methodist Church, have a responsibility that goes far beyond our location and membership. Like the children of Israel, we have been chosen not to a place of privilege, but to a place of responsibility.

After a cup of coffee, we walked out to the "big hole," as one of our children calls it. Bob and I stood at the far southwest corner and looked over the building site. Bob pointed and said, "That's where the Altar will be." I nodded in the affirmative. He kept pointing and speaking. "The choir." "The pulpit." "The baptismal." "The office suites," etc. He spoke with a mixture of pride and warmth about the building that had been designed during the final year of his pastorate. Most of all, Bishop Spain shared his love for the believers of this congregation and his hope for the future of this church.

As we walked back to my office, I had the opportunity to say a word to Bob Spain. As I recall, I said, "Bob, what happened here during your five years as senior pastor is beyond phenomenal. Everyday I realize the depth of your ministry and the extent of your influence. You will never know how much you and Syble are loved by this church and how much you are missed by so many. I want to thank you for the foundation that you laid. I am not you, but I hope that I can keep alive the mystery and hold out the vision for a congregation which continues the work of Christ on earth."

As Bishop Spain turned toward his automobile, he gave me a strong word of encouragement and a healthy pat on the back. I instinctively knew what he meant and he knew what I felt.

As I walked back to my office, I silently called the roll of the distinguished and compassionate pastors and laity who have gone before me. Both the clergy and the laity of the past have left us a lot to do and, with God's help, we will do it.

Why we do it, how we do it, and in whose name we do it is worth pondering.

# Control

At 11:00 AM on November 16th, I saw snow swirling against barren trees and a tumultuous gray sky. It's not supposed to pay a visit until after the Thanksgiving turkey has been carved. Not supposed to come until Christmas draws near.

There was nothing that I could do about it. Could not divert it, turn it off, or wish it away. Could not tell it to wait until a more fitting time. Telling the snow how I felt about its poor timing would have been to no avail.

Life is that way. It takes a lot of unpredictable turns. Life does not always fit into our forecast. It is impossible to anticipate what is around the next corner. Life's timing does not always match our clock. God's clock and ours do not always tell the same time.

An unanticipated snow reminds us that we are not in control of life. It tells us that there are some parts of life that cannot be pushed, manipulated, or harnessed.

I am thankful that I cannot control all that happens in life. If it were up to me, I'd probably make a mess of it. If it were up to me to build a grand design for what happens or does not happen, it would never occur to me to send a lovely snow on November 16th.

How we discern the mind of God in nature, events, others, and ourselves is worth pondering.

# Doing Good for the Sake of Goodness

It was a standing ovation. It was given for Grace and Elwood Denson at the recent session of the Tennessee Conference of the United Methodist Church. The Reverend Denson has been on disability leave from the conference since June 26, 1970. In that year he had a stroke while serving as senior minister of Brentwood United Methodist Church.

Though Elwood has been on disability leave, he has not taken leave from his commitment to the mission and ministry of Brentwood United Methodist Church. He has continued to lead by modeling a distinctive Christian witness. He participates in the P.E.P. Club, the Robert I. Moore Sunday School Class, the Chancel Choir, the exercise class, and he and Grace are often found serving Holy Communion the first Sunday of each month.

But there is something more than what Elwood does. Who Elwood *is* stands out more than what he *does*. He is a person who has remained true, compassionate, and real.

One day last week, Elwood came into my office to say a word to me about Brentwood United Methodist Church and about the recent elections to the General and Jurisdictional Conferences of the United Methodist Church. He displayed a gentleness of manner and a level of thoughtfulness that is, at best, uncommon. And there was that receiving smile which is so characteristic of his demeanor.

At Annual Conference, Grace read the statement that he had written. All of us would do well to listen to it:

"I am grateful to have been a part of this Tennessee Annual Conference for forty-one years. I was able to serve in an active way for nineteen. Serving in the Conference was very fulfilling as I served some of the best churches in the Conference for fifteen years, and Conference Youth Director for four. Also, as camp manager of Beersheba Springs Assembly Grounds for three years after my illness.

"Serving as a delegate to two General and Jurisdictional Conferences was some of the highlights of my career.

"I am grateful that my wife had the opportunity to serve as Associate Director of the Conference Council on Ministries for sixteen years. We felt, as a family, that we were still serving the Conference.

"This Conference has meant so much to us. When illness struck, you were like a family to us. You loved us, supported us, gave us faith and courage to face the given . . . and a way to GIVE and get the most out of life.

"Without you, my family, and God's help, I would never have reached this milestone in my life.

"We pray God's blessing upon this Conference as it continues to carry out the ministry of the church."

I know why the Annual Conference bolted to its feet and thundered with applause. It is because we always respond to people who are steadfast in spite of great odds. We admire and respect people who continue to make a difference even while swimming upstream. Our hearts go out to those who keep on keeping on with a kind of assurance which seems to come from beyond. In Elwood Denson the Conference saw a good pastor, an able administrator, a kind friend, and a devoted servant.

Elwood's life speaks to me about goodness. Goodness, in the best sense of the word, does what is right and selfless without desire for the self-congratulatory fruits of the action. When a person is good for the sake of goodness, it is evident that means and ends are not easily distinguished. And, in my judgment, no good act can produce an evil result. Evil means, even for a good end, produces evil results.

Goodness for the sake of goodness and goodness alone promotes the true business of humankind, which is to be in relation to love and hence to God.

In one account, the Scriptures say that Jesus went about doing good. That's why the throng applauded. Elwood and Grace have gone about doing good.

It's worth pondering.

# The God Who Turns Toward Us

The Old Testament prophets believed that if people did not repent of sin, life would get worse and not better. Refusal to repent would bring about doom and darkness. This means that failure to repent would result in less love in the hearts of people.

On the other hand, these Hebrew prophets believed that if people did repent, life would get better and not worse. Repentance would bring about a "day of the Lord," where persons would be restored to God and to each other.

For the Old Testament writers and for Jesus, repentance was possible because God's love was steadfast. Repentance was not a tit-for-tat transaction. It was possible only because God is already turned toward us, even before we consider turning toward the Holy One.

Thus, we can repent of sin because God has already turned toward us. At the cross God turned toward us. At the resurrection God turned toward us. In the breaking of bread and the serving of wine, God is present to us. In the reading and proclamation of the Word God is revealed to us. In deeds of love and kindness God is shared with us. Thankfully, we can return to the Lord because God graciously leans in our direction. We do not have to get God's attention. We already have it.

Why we do not turn to the One who has already turned toward us is worth pondering.

# Good People

Being a Christian pastor puts me in touch with many good people. I experience people being compassionate, going the extra mile, taking the high road, and being generous without any thought of receiving anything in return.

I hear people say nice words like "thank you," "please," "can I help?" "you are doing a great job!" and "be good to yourself."

I watch people listening to other people; listening behind the words to feelings; listening to hurts, hopes, fears, anxieties, and wishes.

I see people coming to others when there is death, sickness, defeat, or loss. People do reach out. People do care. People are concerned.

To put the matter right in the middle of the table, there are a mountain of good, well-intentioned people in the world.

If there is another side to the coin, it is that people tend to be good until their own self-interest is at stake. When self-interest is threatened, our hand can become a club, our foot can became a weapon, our tongue can become a knife, and our conscience can become compromised.

There are times in life when our self-interest must be put aside for the uplifting of others. It is not easy, but life does call upon us to make sacrifices for others, which is the highest form of love.

It is a sad and terrible commentary on our generation that in spite of all of the good people, more and more of us are letting self-interest override what is best for the family, the community, the nation, and the Church. The demise of the family, the community, the nation, and the Church is more likely when we act out of pure uncompromised self-interest.

It is worth pondering.

# Happiness, the Fruit of Faith

Maybe it is my age, or the time of year, or having just returned from vacation, but I have found myself thinking about what makes for happiness. The culture tells us that we cannot be happy unless we drive a particular car, vacation in a certain place, send our children to a brand name school, live in a popular neighborhood, or chase after a highly chosen career.

We are told by newspaper advertising, TV commercials, mass communication, and a thousand hidden persuaders that we can find happiness if we will search for it. So people search for happiness by chasing down the roads of pleasure, sex, marriage, work, drugs, travel, social service, and even religion.

People who believe that happiness can be sought and found are forever changing things. Changing jobs, wives, moving from one house to another, one community to another, one church to another, as if a change in scenery will provide happiness.

There is a reason that happiness cannot be found by chasing it. The reason is that we carry our happiness or unhappiness inside us. Therefore, we take it into every new situation.

Happiness flows from the inside out and not from the outside in, and that is why people have found it in some very unusual places.

Likewise, happiness does not come from something that we purchase. I have never bought one thing that made me happy. I have bought things that were useful or that gave me pleasure, but "having" does not bring happiness.

Too many people believe that happiness is the goal of life. But the goal of life is not to be happy. If we understand happiness to be the goal of life, we will be forever frustrated and anxious. Rather, the goal of life is to be good, loving, humble, and just. These are the qualities that God would have us to center upon. Happiness, in my judgment, is the by-product of goodness, compassion, humility, and fairness. That is where most of our thought and energy should go if we are to know the joy that comes from within.

So, do not search for happiness. Let it be the by-product of that which is deeply and yet profoundly within us.

It is worth pondering.

# Killing Our Children

I was beyond shock at the mother who apparently murdered her two sons. What brought her to this state has not and may not ever be revealed. In reflecting on that sad incident in Union, South Carolina, I thought about how we unintentionally *kill* our children. To be sure, we do not *murder* them in a physical sense, but unless we are very careful, we can kill their spirit.

For example, we warn our children against addiction to marijuana, cocaine, heroin, or other habit forming drugs, but we do not warn them about other possible dangers. Addiction to beer, cigarettes, junk food, television, video games, automobiles, computers, designer clothes, shopping malls, credit cards, high tech toys, and plastic stuff is not only considered acceptable behavior, but is strongly encouraged by every form of advertising. I feel that we kill the desire to serve humanity by teaching our children that the highest value in life is to be a big consumer. So big is the desire to consume in America that consumer sovereignty and consumer freedom of choice dominate all other human rights—civil, political, and economic.

Furthermore, we have laws in this country against the molestation of children, but we do not have laws against the merchants of hedonism. Bombarding our children with the notion that more things brings more happiness does not help them to come alive—it deadens their spirits.

Likewise, the words that we use with our children can be of a killing sort. Last Friday evening while waiting for a table at a nearby restaurant, I witnessed a father talking to a teenaged son like he was less than human. The father's words were belittling, sharp, cutting, and unbearable to hear. Hearing the words caused me to hurt inside. Too much of that kind of talk will kill a relationship between a father and a son. Our words can hurt or they can heal.

I want us to be aware that what we do or do not do can lead to the spiritual, emotional, or relational death of our children. With the help of God, I want us to understand that we have the wonderful opportunity to help our children to live. I believe that real living is a by-product of loving others, serving others, and keeping one's life open to God. Death sets in when we fail to love, serve, or notice those times when God comes to us. Teach our children these things and they will find life. Teach them the opposite and they will go the way that leads to death.

It is worth pondering.

# Love, Criticism, and Meaning

H. Michael Hartoonian has advanced the notion that the essence of good citizenship is found in the habit of love, the knowledge and practice of criticism, and the search for meaning. Such high values can also be applied to living out the Christian ethos.

Within the concept of love, an important attribute is loyalty. In a word, we cannot truly love a person, the Church, or even God without being loyal. In my judgment, we tend to support that which we love. Conversely, we tend to be disloyal to that which we do not love. Thus, those who love their spouse, their children, their congregation, and God display a natural loyalty.

To reflect critically on life from the vantage point of the Christian faith is also an important ingredient for building life around a Christian ethic. Christians should strive to view life from a point of reference that is to be found in the life, teachings, death, and resurrection of Jesus Christ.

Today, there seems to be a proneness toward superficiality. A depth of critical reflection is lacking. As Pierre Bayle (1697) noted, "Whereas solid and essential reasons which reveal truth are difficult to come by, some people are prone to follow the easier course. Hence, they almost always take the side on which more superficial traits are apparent." It is worth noting that people tend to be lovingly critical of those institutions, ideas, and people in which they find personal meaning. Thus, if we find meaning in life and in Jesus Christ, we will lovingly criticize those institutions, ideas, and people in which we find personal meaning. So, to love is to be both loyal and lovingly critical at the same time.

Finally, meaning is achieved through engagement. Engagement means being intensively involved with God and others in common activities, commonly perceived as good for self, as well as for others so engaged. For a growing number of people, detachment from ultimate concerns has become commonplace. Detachment from the hurts and hopes of others does not bring meaning; it bears the load of meaning's absence. Hiding in the tiny narrow world of self-interest does not bring life; it significantly destroys life.

Knowing that love involves loyalty, that loving criticism is important to finding the truth, and that meaning is achieved through engagement is worth pondering.

# Name for Self

My Sunday morning custom is to leave home early, stop for a big breakfast, and head for the church. On a recent Sunday morning, I sat at the counter of an all-night diner and listened to a man who had made a killing in real estate ventures (twenty-four-hour restaurants are perfect places for plumbing the depths and shallows of the American mind). This man clearly mistook luck for success. No doubt he was lipping full of the confidence which endows mortals. He spoke authoritatively on any and all subjects. He knew why the stock exchange was sluggish. He knew why the University of Tennessee was not winning. He knew why hunger is a daily crisis for some people. He was an authority on politics, international affairs, and religion. He understood why farmers were not making more money, why Koreans were making more money, and why Europeans were not as prosperous as we.

Isn't is strange how gambler's luck can give people the assurance of wisdom for which philosophers search in vain? Because this man had been fortunate in one area, he knew something about everything, and everything about most things.

I pity the man's wife and children. But they probably regard the new house and the trip to Europe as adequate compensation for the task of being convinced by his attempt to make a name for himself.

It's worth pondering.

# Settling Our Differences

On the surface, *Tribute* is a motion picture about a man who is diagnosed with cancer and about his response to that disease. But at a much deeper level, *Tribute* is about a man who is not reconciled to his own son. *Tribute* is about a father and son who needed to settle their differences. Like those characters in this movie, one of the persistent needs of our life is to settle our differences.

There are many ways that we try to settle our differences. Some of us try to settle our differences by taking flight. In so doing, we try to settle our differences by flying away from them. We try to handle our differences by not handling them. We try to settle our differences by ignoring them. We try to settle our differences by putting our heads in the sand like the proverbial ostrich. At other times we try to settle our differences by taking flight with excessive drugs, alcohol, and barbiturates. Taking flight is one of the ways that many of us handle our differences.

Others of us try to handle our differences not by taking flight, but by fighting back. We clench our fists and set our jaws. We practice an eye-for-an-eye and a tooth-for-a-tooth kind of ethics. We harbor a grudge. We act out our resentments, and we believe that every punishment should be equal to every offense.

Still others of us try to settle our differences by traveling the path of compromise. We choose to live in the land of compromise, whose primary symbol is a very high tolerance level for those who differ from us. The spirit of compromise has its place, but at times, compromise can keep us from dealing creatively with differences that exist between ourselves and others.

Matthew 5: 17–26 speaks to us about two ways to handle our differences. The first is to learn to live by the ethics of a higher righteousness. According to this higher ethic, it is not only wrong to murder, it is also wrong to hate.

This Scripture lesson indicates another way for us to settle our differences. Said Matthew, "So if you are offering your gift at the altar, and there remember that your brother has something against you, leave your gift there before the altar and go; first be reconciled to your brother and then come and offer your gift." According to this, being reconciled to one another is far more important than whatever gift one might leave at the altar.

Settling the differences that exist between people is crucial. And such differences can be settled if we live by the higher righteousness and seek to be reconciled to each other. If we do not live by a higher standard and seek reconciliation, our differences will not go away. Instead, they will fester and grow until we are separated more and more from others, from ourselves, and, ultimately, from God.

It's worth pondering.

# The Inner Life

I t's not difficult to define some things. It's easy to define work, colors, shapes, objects, places, people, and things. But it's not so easy to define what it means to live the Christian life. The Christian way of life is much too important a thing to be defined. Other things may be defined with impunity, but not the Christian life.

The Christian way of life is meant to be lived, and out of the experience of living it will come clarity. The Christian life can be represented by words, but these words are often not understood by one not living the Christian life. Such words become passwords among family members, but they are like shorthand for those beyond the faith.

There once lived a "knight of faith" in Denmark. It was often rumored that there was no greater Christian in all of Denmark than this noble knight. Spies were sent out to discover how he lived and what he said. Yet, all they found was a "complacent burgher" who could not be distinguished from his neighbors by the way he looked, talked, or conducted his life. The spies returned saying that the knight could not be distinguished from others by his outer life.

The spies went to a wise Christian to determine how they were to know what it was that made the knight such a great Christian. The wise old believer instructed his questioners not to look to the outward forms, whether saintly or common, but to the inward "movements of infinity" that have no outward expression.

What distinguished that knight from all others is something so deep and personal that it cannot be outwardly observed or directly communicated—and that is—the Christian life is discerned and fostered by its substance and not its form.

It is this difficult to define *substance* that has much to do with the Christian life. Our Wesleyan heritage teaches us that it is the spirit or inner principle of Christ's life that becomes in us the Christian life.

Our life is a Christian life when we identify, recognize, focus on, and draw close to this Life—the Holy One—who comes to us.

It is this inward riveting of our two lives that allows Him to be Christ and us to be Christians; Him to live his Christ-life and us to live our Christian lives.

So, the outer form of our Christian lives may differ radically (and at times confusingly). But our inner lives must converge on God so that the two become one.

How that happens is worth pondering.

# Trash Talk

Trash talk TV is a problem. Much of it is an exhibition of outrageous, bizarre, and often deviant behavior that is aired under the guise of entertainment and enlightenment. Through these programs viewers learn something of the downside of human nature. If these shows depicted improvement in the human condition, they would run the risk of losing a portion of the audience.

I also worry about some of talk radio, because much of it leaves those who are being talked about in a defenseless position. For example, if someone decided to slander me on talk radio and if I was unaware of the content of the program, I could not make an explanation of my view. Serious damage has been done to people by persons who have nothing to lose. This way of communicating is not an example of "do unto others as you would have them do unto you."

At a more everyday level I am concerned about the lack of respect and courtesy that is evidenced in everyday speech.

So many children came to our house on Halloween that we almost ran out of treats. Very few said, "Thank you." Only two of the children said, "Sir." "Yeah" and "Nawh" were the expressions of choice. More than one child addressed me as. "Hi, Dude." When I put the candy in one child's sack, the youngster responded by saying "Cheap." There was not much evidence of deference, courtesy, or respect for the generosity and feelings of others.

In many adults, graciousness in speech is absent. Talking down to each other is accepted. Talking *about* instead of *with* each other is commonplace. The courtesy of warm loving speech is like a foreign language to many people.

I am concerned about how we talk, because words shape reality, and our speech can hurt or it can heal. As we follow Christ, we should work overtime to use language that helps and heals, rather than words that show no consideration for the feelings of others.

In writing to the Church at Colossae Paul said, "Let your speech always be gracious, seasoned with salt, so that you may know how to answer everyone."

Why we need to be gracious in our speaking is worth pondering.

# What Is It to Be a Christian?

**W**hat is it to be a Christian? What are the pains and the joys? What is the price that is to be paid for being born into a Christian family, for belonging to a Christian Church, for choosing the Christ way of life for themselves?

This is an important question, because we are now living in a culture that is increasingly non-Christian. That is to say, we are living in a time when religious values no longer permeate our homes, workplaces, neighborhoods, or the world community. It is harder and more difficult to be a Christian because the culture militates against, rather than supports, our being Christian.

We are now subject to all wind and weather, all the tides and currents, and all the impact and erosion of the outside world.

Old loyalties are now being washed away. We are tempted and seduced to be like the general public.

We no longer have the protection of the Christian ghetto. Our Jewish neighbors found this to be true! When they lived in the ghettos of New York, for example, they could keep the life of Judaism in an easier fashion. But, when the ghettos broke up, it was more difficult to practice the faith of Judaism.

For Christians of yesterday it was easier to be a Christian, because they were padded with an armor that made them impregnable in a world of enemies. Being a Christian was supported by family and community. Not so today!

Today, many Christians have no core beliefs. Everything has eroded. Our inner forces have evaporated. Our inner resistance has been reduced to nil. We have been flattened out. The desire to be like others has compromised our faith.

It is worth pondering.

# Standing over against Evil

The Tuesday, June 18, issue of *The Tennessean* reported that "Fires have destroyed thirty-six black churches across the South over the last eighteen months." As sad and terrible as these destructive forces happen to be, it is impossible to destroy a Church. A building can be burned out, but a Church cannot be extinguished. A Christian Church is composed of people who believe that Christ is Lord. It is a community of persons who worship the God of Jesus of Nazareth. Its message is the Good News that the grace displayed in the life and teachings of Jesus is available to all persons, and that such love is the basis for the redemption of humankind. Its ethic is rooted in what love requires of all persons. Its hope is in the final triumph of righteousness. Its fellowship is open to people of all ages, races, and nations. It stands firmly against evil, injustice, and oppression in whatever forms they present themselves. It believes that there is no place where God is not. This—and much more—is what the Church is, and it cannot be destroyed by fire, threat, terror, or crucifixion.

The building where the Church gathers for worship, study, and prayer can be burned in the dark of night, but the Church cannot and will not be eliminated from the landscape of any community.

Those who burn church buildings must be striking out against the believers who gather in such buildings for the worship of God! They do so with the false notion that intimidation, fear, and destruction have the power to both silence and break the spirit of a people. However, the reverse is true. With every fire, there is a new determination to be the community of faith. With every "crucifixion," there is yet another resurrection. With every blaze leaping into the night sky, there is a brighter and stronger fire burning in the hearts of those who understand the true nature and purpose of the Church. For every arsonist, there are untold numbers who believe that love is stronger than the threat of death.

Every time I read about another building going down in flames, I make a new resolve to stand over against the evil that moves people toward destroying the places where African-Americans profess their faith in Jesus Christ. In the name of Christ we must do all that we can to help with the rebuilding of these buildings.

We will be a better and stronger people if we will speak out against racism, in whatever fashion it presents itself.

It is worth pondering.

# Simply Not Funny

One of God's good gifts is the yearning for a hearty laugh. Laughter can be good medicine. A chuckle can make the load a bit lighter. Often the source of laughter contains a touch of wisdom. Some recent gatherings include the following.

A person visiting a nursing home inquired of a 92-year-old resident, "Can you tell me my name?" The kind, elderly lady replied, "No sir, but if you will go up to the desk, they will tell you."

Most congregations are full of volunteer types. They will volunteer someone else for almost anything.

A parishioner asked her pastor to officiate at a funeral for her dog. The preacher stood fast and said that he did not do funerals for dogs. The lady said that she was going to give $10,000 to the building fund in memory of her pet if he would give the dog a proper burial. "Oh," said the preacher, "you did not tell me that you had a Methodist dog."

What do you get when you play country music backwards? You get your wife back, job back, truck back, and you sober up.

If you are beginning to encounter some hard bumps, be glad. At least you are out of the rut.

The trouble with a person who works like a horse is that all he or she wants to do in the evenings is hit the hay.

Marriage is like the Army—most everyone complains, but you'd be surprised at how many reenlist.

The optimist is often as wrong as the pessimist, but he or she is far happier.

The real measure of a person's wealth is how much he or she would be worth if all of his or her money were lost.

Love is the one and only asset that competition cannot undersell or destroy.

The most valuable thing you can learn from experience is not to rely on it.

Probably the most difficult of all instruments to play is second fiddle.

Sign on a church: "Try one of our Sundays."

Sign on a hospital: "Give blood, it was meant to be circulated."

Sign in a church meeting room: "After all is said and done, more is said than done."

Sign in a schoolroom: "The cornerstone of wisdom is laid when a person finally gets wise on herself or himself."

Sign on a child's tricycle: "Tot rod."

Since laughter is such an important part of life, I have the feeling that Jesus must have had a good sense of humor. Many of his sayings point to a dry wit, which must have caused those who listened to unclench the fist and to ride light in the saddle. He was no sourpuss.

A good laugh is essential to a balanced life, but it should never be at the expense of someone else. That's why ethnic jokes are out of place and inappropriate for the followers of Jesus who demonstrate God's love for all persons. Ethnic jokes say more about the teller than about the object of the joke.

It's worth pondering.

# The Church

# How Big Should a Church Be?

The question, "How big should a church be?" is one that occasionally surfaces in the life of a congregation. For some, that is an honest question. For others, it is a way of saying, "I feel left out." Either way it is a question that deserves an answer.

In the first place, the Church of Jesus Christ should never put a sign in the yard or send a nonverbal message that the congregation is for "members only." Nor should we, as Christ's Body, say to ourselves or to nonbelievers that we have all of the members that we need, and that others should find another congregation in which to profess Christ.

Second, it is important that we carefully scrutinize our motives for reaching out for new people. If Brentwood United Methodist is wanting new persons for what they can do for the institutional church, we are committing the sin of using people. Using people to meet institutional needs is a sad and terrible thing.

If, however, we are responding to persons because we believe that they need to worship God, learn of Christ, serve others in the Lord's name, and have their brokenness healed, then we have a responsibility to be open to all who will come.

Reading the history of Brentwood United Methodist Church will clearly demonstrate that this congregation long ago decided to meet the spiritual needs of a growing community. Conversely, there are congregations in this and every area which have consciously or unconsciously decided not to offer Christ to a rapidly multiplying population. To be the Body of Christ for more and more people is not easy. It requires a big heart, which encompasses a strong element of sacrifice and service.

When Peter preached to a crowd of people, the book of Acts says, "So those who welcomed his message were baptized, and that day about three thousand persons were added."

Should Peter have said, "Sorry, but three thousand happens to be too many"? Rather, the believers in Acts took on the more difficult task of helping those three thousand to become the Church of Jesus Christ.

Helping a large-membership congregation to become a real Church is not easy. For this to happen, it is very important for every person to have a task, belong to a group, and to be held accountable for spiritual growth. Persons who belong to "congregations within the congregation," usually feel at home no matter what the numerical size.

Third, there is no magical number that indicates an exact numerical size. Rather, we should preach the Word and offer the sacraments to all who stand in need. Those who accept and respond must, in the name of Christ, be welcomed into the community of faith. When persons respond, we must give all that we can, and do all that we can, and love all that we can so that they and we might be nurtured in Christ's way of life.

Finally, a congregation's bigness should not be determined by how many people are listed on the roll. Bigness should be judged by the depth of our spirituality, our eagerness to display Christ to all who will listen, and our willingness to promote justice among all of God's people. Bigness is not a number; it is a willingness to give ourselves to others for the sake of Christ.

I have pastored congregations of fifty members, seventy-five members, 325 members, 750 members, 2,300 members, and now 3,800 members. In each of those congregations I have wanted the church to be distinctively evangelistic, socially concerned, and welcoming to all who would come. In the words of John Wesley, I have wanted the church to "spread scriptural holiness throughout the land." I have held fast to the belief that any who come should be provided worship, nurture, and opportunities for service and healing.

How many is not the question. No matter what a congregation's numerical size is—large or small—it must follow the example of Christ of never losing sight of each individual. Whether we are being faithful to Christ by being responsive to all people is the question.

How and when we offer the Gospel to any and all is worth pondering.

# Is It True? or How Can I Benefit?

As time passes, questions change. Thirty years ago when I became a pastor, the primary faith question was "Is it true?" College students, farmers, teachers, scientists, homemakers, and others wanted to know the truth as presented by Christianity. Study groups, classes, conferences and conversations went on and on around concerns about the convictions and claims of Christianity.

The atmosphere was so alive with such questions that I did a doctoral thesis that aimed at determining what people believe, and how the Church through preaching and education could help clarify and strengthen the beliefs of people.

Today, the assumptions seem to have shifted. In the Church, as in much of life, "Who benefits?" is more important than the validity of certain beliefs.

It is a sad and terrible thing that many people want to join congregations that can be of benefit. So the primary question becomes, "How can the Church benefit me?" If that is the most important question, people will "shop" for congregations that can provide the most.

If local congregations buy into this mentality, the temptation will be to market the Church like a secular product. Concepts like the marketing strategy, tactics, control, new products, new ideas, cost management, target market selection, target response and service strategy, promotion, demographics, public relations, and consulting services will become a part of our everyday life.

Our purpose is not to market the institutional Church like one would market a new restaurant. We have a larger purpose. That purpose is to help connect persons to God and each other through Jesus Christ. To be sure, we need to do that in ways that are understandable and meaningful, but we cannot "sell" the Gospel. We can only bear witness to its power to change life.

Therefore, what we believe about God and what God wants to do through us is more important than "How can I benefit?"

It is worth pondering.

# Knowing and Following Jesus

Observing life and listening closely can be very revealing. Such was the case last week. While strolling through the foyer of the church, I overheard a woman saying to a child, "The church is where we are taught the religion about Jesus." Her observation set my mind to spinning. Now that I have reflected on that women's statement, I am not certain that she was on target.

It is here that we teach the religion of Jesus as distinguished from the religion about Jesus. To be certain, there is much in Christianity that is about Jesus—things said of and believed concerning Jesus, theories to account for Him, and accumulated explanations and interpretations of him.

The larger task is to introduce people to the religion of Jesus—the religion which Jesus himself possessed and by which He lived. His filial fellowship with God. His purity, unselfishness, sincerity, sacrifice, His exaltation of spiritual values, and His unqualified love of others.

There is a vast difference in knowing about Jesus and in truly falling under the spell of the Master's life and influence.

That difference is worth pondering.

# Two Ways at the Same Time

If "hell" means separation from God, the world in which we live is stuck in what the ancient Hebrews called "sheol." Our social, domestic, and personal problems are scaling the heights. Within the Church I hear two approaches to these vexing troubles.

For example, there are many who feel that such problems lie wholly outside the Church's mission. They understand the religious enterprise as pertaining exclusively to God, and the soul, and to eternity. Church is a place to get away from the agonies of life, not a place to struggle with them.

I have had people say to me that they came to church to forget their problems. Said one such person, "What I want in this sanctuary is a moratorium on complexity. I want to hear about the majesty of God and what I have to look forward to in the next life. I wish you would preach more on the book of Revelation and when the end is going to come. That is what excites me—when this whole sorry mess of history is going to be over and we get to the place of peace and joy."

Therein lies one answer to our question.

At the other end of the spectrum are people who would say that solving problems such as family life, crime, racism, mental illness, moral failure, sexism, and addictions are within the framework of the Church's purpose.

These people get restless with "God talk" that does not scratch where people itch. Rituals of worship and prayer that do not connect with real life are of little value. Such persons say that if the Church cannot provide these tools, they will turn away from an institution that is irrelevant. These people do not want to turn the Church into a forum for political, social, and personal problems, but they do want the teachings of Jesus to apply to the real lives of real people.

These two extremes can be found in most congregations today, and they are not unique to American religion. I would say that religion needs to go in both directions at the same time. Our Christianity must feed the soul, while not neglecting the daily down-to-earth issues and needs that face the frailty of the human condition. To have one without the other is just not good practical Methodism.

It's worth pondering.

# What the Church Must Not Teach

A couple of weeks ago I drove through the neighborhood in which I was reared. When I was growing up we called our part of town "Pinch," because most everyone in that section of the city was "in a pinch." Though we were not poor, many families in Pinch struggled to make the house note and to pay the light bill. Making ends meet was a nagging problem.

Jackson Avenue Methodist Church provided a ministry to those of us who did not have it as easy as we have it today. Our congregation had an empowering message for those who were everything but affluent.

Congregations located in affluent communities now face a different challenge. What kind of message should the Church have for those for whom it has become harder and harder to have three or more cars, two VCRs, a place on the lake, and huge closets stuffed with more clothing that one can possibly wear?

The Church of Jesus Christ must not say that our lives will be more fulfilled, our marriage will be stronger, our families will be happier if we get one more VCR, or a better car, or a bigger and longer trip. It is unacceptable for the Church to teach that our society is a vast supermarket of desire in which each of us is encouraged to stand alone and go out and get what the world owes us.

In both affluent and poor communities, the Church must teach that life takes on meaning not because of what we have or do not have, but because of who we are. Life takes on meaning when we are faithful to our promises, love our enemies, tell the truth, honor the poor, love one another, and continue the work of Christ on earth.

It's worth pondering.

# Inside and Outside of the Church

Difficult-to-answer questions find a way of banging away in my head. One such question surfaced today while I was engaged in spiritual reading. It was, "Are we more influenced by what we learn outside the faith community or what we learn inside the Church?"

Inside the Church we learn that people can be changed by practicing the presence of God. Outside the Church we are taught that who we have been in the past is who we will be in the future.

Inside the Church we learn that we are to love all people as brothers and sisters because God is the parent of us all. Outside the Church we are taught that select people are to be loved.

Inside the Church we learn that we are to be fair and honest because God is just and fair. Outside the Church we learn that cheating is acceptable.

Inside the Church we are taught to practice forgiveness. Outside the Church we are taught to get even.

Inside the Church we are taught to be servants of a just and compassionate God. Outside the Church we are taught to be servants of ourselves.

Inside the Church we learn that sin is not only to be forgiven; it is also to be overcome. Outside the Church we are taught that sin is acceptable as long as you do not get caught.

Inside the Church we are taught to work tirelessly to bring the social order into conformity with the justice of God and the mind of Christ. Outside the Church we are taught to conform to the prevailing notions of what is right and what is wrong.

It is worth pondering.

# Participation and Purpose

Perhaps I am a bit odd, but I find myself continuously reflecting on the purpose of things. At one time I belonged to a service organization for a period of two years. For the entire twenty-four months I puzzled about the purpose of that group. After two years of reflecting, I decided to terminate my relationship to the organization, because I never could figure out what that particular crowd was trying to do. Furthermore, I was baffled about why I continued to stay with an organization whose purpose I did not understand. Since I could not get hold of that purpose, I decided to let others enjoy doing whatever it was they were trying to do.

Makes me wonder if some folks participate in the Church without understanding its purpose.

Let us never have erased from our memory that the Church is the Body of Christ, and that we, as believers, are members of that Body. Since we are the Body of Christ, our purpose is to continue the work of Christ on earth.

How we as a congregation continue the work of Christ in this community in the year of our Lord 1989 is certainly worth pondering.

# The Cross

# No Time or Place

After her aunt had been committed to her final resting place at the old Mudville Cemetery, she wanted to locate the grave of her grandmother who was buried in the same hallowed ground. No one had been there for years, so it was difficult to scratch the memory for the right location. Some of the relatives thought it was to the east; some thought it to the west. No one was certain. As we walked along the grass-covered knoll, we looked for the right location. We passed marker after marker with names and dates stamped in the cold grey stone.

As we searched, I wondered why she wanted to view the stone. Was it to get in touch with childhood memories? Or was it to recall the goodness of a saintly woman? Or was it to link with what her grandmother had left all of us to do?

Or was it to remember how rich she was in some things, while being simple in other ways?

Or did she want to revisit her grandmother's grave because she was known to be a believer?

Today, ninety-some percent answer a Gallop Poll as having at least a generic "belief in God." People will say, "I believe" (*credo* in Latin) to refer to God on Sunday, and again on Monday to express their opinions about the weather or the next election, or whatever. But gentle, loving, humble belief cannot be taken so casually.

The notion of be-lieve is rooted in the Old English *leof*, meaning "dear, cherished, loved, or longed for." Add the prefix "be" (meaning "to cause to be") and what we cherish causes our be-ing—makes us who we are. Therefore, in believing we become what we long for.

I have yet to ask her, but maybe that is the reason that she wanted to stand in front of the stone—to reach back and get in touch with the spirit of a person who knew what should be held dear, cherished, loved, and longed for.

At this season of the year we stand before another symbol—not a grass-covered grave in a cemetery like Mudville—but a cross. Between now and Easter we will survey the wondrous cross. We will stand before it. Look at it. Touch it. Like Janene going to her grandparents' grave, we must revisit the cross lest we forget the One from Nazareth who "cherished, loved, and longed for God" so much that he was willing to sacrifice Himself, that we might experience the God who is far beyond us, but deep within us.

After a bit of searching we found the location of the earth-encased coffin. As we stood there, holding hands, with the wind kissing our faces, we got in touch with a sacrificial love that is not limited to time or place. Such is the cross.

It is worth pondering.

# The Front Line

This morning, I went into a nearby fast-food restaurant to get a cup of coffee. As I was waiting for service, I said to the manager, "Got them organized today?" Quick as a wink, he replied, "We're in good shape—we have a good front line on duty."

I have a long-time friend who has a very successful restaurant business. It's been one of those high volume, low overhead kinds of operations. Excellent real food. By real food I mean vegetables, cornbread, meat, gravy, and rich, rich homemade desserts. I recently had the opportunity to ask him an important question. I said, "Lynn, how have you been so successful?" His answer was unexpected. He did not say "the atmosphere," "the food," or "the location." Without blinking he said, "the waitresses." Many of his waitresses have been with him for as many as fifteen to twenty-five years. They know customers by name. They know how to wait on tables. They know how to work with people. Those long-time servants represent his front line. No matter who is in the kitchen, if the front line is not fitting in and working out, the entire operation will split and flounder.

Coaches know the importance of the front line. The best point guard will not make his strongest contribution without a gifted front line. The most athletic quarterback will not produce for the team if the front line is weak and slow.

Educators know this. A brilliant administration will not amount to much without gifted and compassionate teachers in the classroom. Educational systems are measured by what is taught and learned in the classrooms. It's the front line that is ultimately important.

Pastors know this. Pastors know that the laity reflect the front line of the church. Believers at home, on the street, at work, and at play are where the rubber meets the road. If the living Christ is not witnessed to by front line laity, His influence will be, at best, minimal.

Lent speaks to us about a front line God. When God wanted to communicate love, God displayed himself in human form. God, in Jesus, "dwelt among us full of grace and full of truth. He became all we are that we might become as he is."

Christianity is about front line stuff. It's about a man named Jesus, who loved God and who was a friend to the poor and outcast. It is about those who believe that in Jesus, God spoke a word. A word that leads to life and life abundant. It is about those who have taken the teachings of Jesus and have applied them to the everydayness of life. It is about those who know that they have been forgiven.

Right now our eyes and hearts are turning toward the cross of Christ. In ancient times the cross was a symbol of shame. Common criminals were put to death in this way. It was on a cross that Jesus was put to death—treated by the Roman authorities as a troublemaker. But God took the "symbol of shame" and made it the emblem of hope when he brought forth the resurrection. That which had been the symbol of evil was made the hope of the world.

That, in my judgement, is front line stuff and is worth pondering.

# The Milk Machine

As soon as I sat down the waitress brought me a cup of coffee, a "cafe blanc" creamer, and a glass of water with three chunks of floating ice. After a few moments of fumbling, I found a way to peel back the stuck creamer top, before settling in to a prolonged cup of brew. As usual, one cup called for another.

My waitress did not return. I waited. I drank the water and continued to wait. Impatiently, I looked around the room in hopes of "catching her eye."

Caffeine was crying out for more caffeine. I motioned for another waitress. She said that she could not serve me because it was not her station. I asked her to send my waitress along with a pot of hot coffee. She nodded, but made no promises.

In due time my waitress came bouncing over to the table with coffee and an apology. She said, "I'm sorry about the coffee, but I was busy cleaning the milk machine." She was very busy, but she was consumed by the wrong priority. The milk machine had taken precedent over those whom she had been hired to serve.

The cross of Christ will not let us forget the importance of sacrificial service to those for whom Christ died. But, if we are not careful, we, as the Body of Christ, will spend more effort on the milk machine than on serving.

It's worth pondering.

# Fear

# Anxiety

At least one wag has said that "the curse of anxiety is that it takes itself too seriously." It is true that none of us will escape having a first-hand experience with anxiety. None of us will always live in the salad days of independence, prosperity, and success.

Various seeds produce the plant of anxiety.

It arises out of a sense of loss. Loss of a significant relationship, or a job, or location can be the source of great anxiety.

It also comes from feeling trapped. Only anxiety can come from feeling trapped by a relationship, or an addiction, or a career, or circumstances, or whatever!

Those who feel the stifling of creativity often feel anxious. It is not peaceful not to be able to let the creative juices flow.

The unethical life and the fear of being found out can produce a nightmare of the soul so profound that it will cause the foundations to shake.

And trembling anxiety overtakes us when our resources to cope with life begin to fail us.

If we are to handle our anxieties we must, first, face them. Put a label on them. Call them by a name. Acknowledge their power. That's the first step.

Wise people know the importance of putting themselves in the hands of friends, pastors, counselors, and professional caregivers.

Anyone who has tramped the road of anxiety knows that the more anxieties are denied, the bigger they become.

I Peter tells us to handle our anxieties by casting them on the Lord. It sounds simple, but there is great truth in this advice.

When we cast our burdens upon the Lord, we acknowledge that there are spiritual resources that are far greater than our resources. Countless people have turned to this vast pool of spiritual resources and have found significant assistance. The disciplines of prayer, Bible study, worship, partaking of the sacraments, and contemplation can help even the most skeptical to work through even the most burdensome anxiety.

When we cast our burdens upon the Lord, we become concerned about how God wants things to be and not how we want them to be. Believers know that

God is "with us" as we face, work through, and rise above anxieties. Not to turn to this resource is to be remiss.

It's worth pondering.

# Living with Uncertainty

We are fast losing the ability to talk with each other in meaningful ways. Creative and interesting conversation is becoming a lost art. Since we no longer know how to enjoy plain conversation, we have turned to specialists. In days gone by, many of the problems that we now take to a specialist were solved with compassionate conversation.

I believe that we need to learn how to live with uncertainty, because everyone has a major dilemma in their lives. Everyone has a load to carry and a burden to bear. No one escapes having to handle something that is difficult. The question that I raise is this: are these problems only for specialists, or are they the stuff of ordinary life?

Please do not hear me discounting trained professionals, because I know from personal experience the great help that they can provide.

How can we live in a world like ours without being sad or angry or upset? Should we try to take the pain away, or should we help people to bear their pain? Pain is present because limitations and finitude are not abnormalities. They are part of life, and they are opportunities for us to be open to God.

One of the reasons that we do not share our pain is because we are afraid for people to know us as we really are. We fear that people will not like us if they see us as we are. Where is the grace in that approach to life?

It is worth pondering.

# The Greatest of All Fears

All of us are acquainted with fear, but not all of us have the same fears. We are afraid of not having it all, not reaching perfection, not making more money, not becoming famous, not getting prettier or smarter, not being important, not counting in the eyes of others, not making a difference, not being adored, not being in control, not being appreciated, or not being loved.

The fear of being too busy is, for many of us, a real concern. We are always in the rush hour. Running on high octane is our normal speed. Many of us are too busy to sit down and read a good book or spend one-on-one time with our children.

We fear becoming too selfish or too cynical. When we are too selfish, our fists are more closed than open. And when we are too cynical, our minds are not open to new understandings.

I believe that many of us fear for those whom we love. Will they be hit by a drunken driver? What if a life-threatening disease should be discovered? Is "making the grade" a possibility, or is it out of the question? Will our loved ones experience broken relationships and moral failures? Fear creeps into our hearts as we think about how much we love those whom we love.

On the cultural side, we fear the consequences of racism, sexism, or classism. We know that these do not build up love, but carry the seeds of our demise. We fear the possibility that reconciliation is not a possibility!

It is important that we handle our fear with great care, because it can be so debilitating and powerful that it can lead us to put our confidence in the most unsatisfying places.

As we approach 1996, we need to remember that there is a word more powerful than our fears. Our fears are not likely to disappear, but there is a Biblical notion that is stronger than our human fear. It is faith in a God who says, "Do not fear, for I am with you, do not be afraid, for I am your God; I will strengthen you and I will help you. I will hold you with my right hand" (Isaiah 41:10). Could it be that the fear to trust God is the greatest fear of all?

It is worth pondering.

# Trusting Our Regrets to God

I cannot remember how many times I have placed my hands on a casket and said, "For as much as the departed has entered into life immortal we, therefore, commit his (or her) body to its final resting place, remembering how Jesus said upon the cross, 'Father, into Thy hands I commit my spirit'"

Though I have stood by many a coffin and have prayed with a large number of dying persons, I am not able to put myself in the position of those who are about to depart this life.

Could it be that we bear more than pain and sorrow when we are departing this life?

I expect that one of the heaviest burdens for a dying person is regret. Regret about conflicts unresolved. Regret about breached relationships not healed. Regret about potential unfulfilled. Regret about promises not kept, and years that will never be lived.

When we come to that time when we shall "cross the bar" there will be unfinished business. Only the very old will escape this "unfinished business" feeling.

The greater our purposes, the more we love others, the more we savor the goodness of everyday life, the more life has been an adventure—the more we will regret. We will regret not having more of what we have highly treasured.

When I come to those dying moments, I hope I can trust my regrets to God's care and mercy.

What other choices do we have?

It is worth pondering.

# Forgiveness

# Not One or the Other, but Both

As followers of Jesus Christ, we live with God's commandments and with God's forgiveness. When we are assured, overconfident, and curved in upon ourselves, we are brought face-to-face with the commandments of Christ. Settling in our hearts are commandments like "love thy neighbor as thyself"; "do unto others as you would have them to do unto you"; "love the Lord thy God with all of thy heart, soul, mind, and strength"; "do not remove the mote from the eye of others without removing the log from your own eye"; "forgive not seven, but seventy times seven"; etc. Learning and living the commandments of Christ keeps us in right relationship to God and to each other.

On the other hand, when we fail, sin, and hurt others or God, we need to experience the loving forgiveness of Christ. None of us happens to be made out of steel. Feet of clay are the common lot of humanity. Sins of omission and sins of commission are with every breathing person. Thoughts, words, and deeds, which separate us from God, each other, and ourselves, are ingrained in the soul of every person. No one is removed from fallenness. When we are broken and fail, we need to experience God's love.

In my judgment the Church needs to proclaim and live out both the commandments of Christ (law) and the love of Christ (gospel). Law without gospel can lead to harsh legalism. Gospel without law can become permissive.

We need to remember that the commandments of Christ have not been defeated by the cross, and that the love of Christ continues to be present to all who stand in need.

# When Life Doesn't Come Out Right

L ast Friday morning I served Holy Communion to ninety-six members of the Sonshine Choir, just before they boarded two buses and two vans for their "Texas Tour." As we were leaving the sanctuary, one of the parents said, "I hope everything comes out right."

Therein lies a desire that all of us have. We like for things to come out right. Whether we are building a birdhouse, or putting in plumbing to an outdoor spigot, we like for everything to fit.

This notion started in our early childhood. One of our first toys was likely a set of blocks of some sort. With these we learned to get a sense of order, a sense of decency, a sense of rightness, a sense of fitting here, and not fitting there.

We like for things to come out right. We want our little payments to come out even, and we go through life living with this principle. The last thing that is done for us, the digging of our grave, is done with mathematical regard for precise dimensions.

But one of the strange things, and yet not so strange, is that the more we love order, and the more we like for things to come out right, the more highly frustrated we are when we are unable to make things fit.

I saw a child in our preschool who was pounding a stack of blocks with a wooden hammer because she could not make them stack up just right. All of us know how it is to come home and get along miserably with all the members of the family, simply because things would not come out right at work.

Carry this a little further. We not only want our blocks to fit, and our coffins to fit, we also want life to come out right—right for us. And most of us are willing to pay a fantastic price to make sure that life comes out as we have perceived it, prejudged it, and attempted to prearrange it. We will make most any sacrifice to be sure that a given venture comes just as we would wish it to come, and ends on schedule just as we wish it to end.

I know people who have lived this way for so long that, for them, a vacation is impossible. They carry the precise moment of arrival and departure at every place they intend to pass. They make a burden and an agony out of all of life's short journeys, assuming, I am sure, that some virtue is gathered by staying on precise schedule, so that when all is totaled at the end of the line, life will come out all right.

But wise people know that life does not always come out right. It does not fit into tight little grooves. No matter how hard we try, life will not come out right—and this is the value of forgiveness.

It's worth pondering.

# God

# Discerning the Presence of God

Discerning the presence of God is both easy and difficult. It is difficult because of all of the evil that we witness every day of our lives. No one needs to document that fact. Wrongdoing and unreality are spread out before us in every issue of every newspaper. But we also know that sinfulness is not only "out there"—it also resides within us. Discerning God's presence in our sinfulness is not easy, but it is possible because God is forever coming to us and clinging to our indifference in the hope that someday our needs, or at least our tragedies, will waken us to respond to God's advances.

On the other side is the fact that discerning God's activity is not so difficult. God's presence is everywhere: in Brentwood, on the banks of the Little Harpeth River, in the traffic on Franklin Road, in the stores, in every inch of every room, in every house, in the hospital—in the patients' rooms, in the intensive care unit, in the waiting room, and at the snack bar. There is not any place in all of creation where God is not.

We do not have to go to some special place, assume some unique position, or be gathered in some special assembly in order to find God, reach God, or talk to God. No matter where we are we can unburden ourselves before the Lord. No matter where we find ourselves we can discern God's presence. Discerning God's activity is a matter of being intentional, being aware, and being open to the Holy in the midst of the profane.

It is worth pondering.

# A Little Girl Asked . . .

As a pastor, I receive many questions about this and that. Most every question from the "river to the railroad" seems to float to my desk. Some inquiries are practical, some personal, and some theological.

Often, the most provocative and the most difficult questions come from children. Adults, as they grow older, seem to lose the capacity to wonder, to dream, to search, and to question.

After a recent Sunday service a little girl asked, "What is God like?" What a question! Perhaps the biggest question of all. How does one answer in a practical, easy-to-understand way?

One could give the answer provided by Anselm, "God is that than which nothing greater can be conceived." Or, one could give the answer offered by Paul Tillich, "God is our ultimate concern." Or, one could give the answer of a philosopher and say that God is like that which is both transcendent and imminent.

Or, one could be like the ancient Hebrews who would not use the word "God," because to place the word God on human lips could be to profane God. So, the Israelite people developed a word for God that they called YHWH or "Yahweh."

Or, a person could use street talk about God and refer to the Holy One as "the man upstairs," as if one were talking about a divine bellhop of sorts. Street talk sees the Deity as the great "Someone who looks after me." A noted movie star referred to God as "my heavenly chum."

The Bible uses many metaphors to talk about what God is like. According to the Biblical record, God is like a creator, judge, spirit, father, mother, shepherd, king, ruler, lord, master, etc.

All of these images give us a clue as to what God is like, but they are "hard put" to answer the question of the little girl who stood in the foyer of the church with Sunday School literature in hand.

To push the issue further, does it really matter how we conceive of God? Does it have anything to do with how we live, how we relate to others, and how we make it through life? In my judgment it matters in an ultimate way. If, for example, we see God as the "man upstairs," God could become too human-like, too chummy, too utilitarian. In this image God exists primarily to serve us, and not the reverse.

Still, the question hangs: how do we answer the wide-eyed child who stands outside the sanctuary door, clad in a pretty dress, with a tiny bow in her hair? How does the preacher put the answer in language that she can understand and hold on to for all the days of her life. How do I say it so she can absorb it, make sense of it and be guided by it every day of her life?

I am going to try to answer the child's question in Sunday's sermon. Maybe I will and maybe I will not. But I am going to try, because how we think of God determines how we think about ourselves and how we think about each other.

It's worth pondering.

# Being Still, Knowing God

Being busy is not a virtue. But that is what people say—"busy." Bump into people almost any place and inquire, "How are you?" Nine times out of ten they will reply, "busy" or "busy busy." A sense of hurry pervades much of life. Last Wednesday evening I was standing outside the classroom where a course is being taught on "The Hurried Family." As people came out of the class, I overheard a wife say to her husband, "Please hurry or we will never make it." Right after a class devoted to hurry in a hurried world!

This compulsion to hurry is so acute that it is possible to be uncomfortable when we are not going lickety-split. One of our parishioners said that the only time she gives herself to stop is while others are being served Holy Communion on the first Sunday of each month. It is the only time that some people reflect, meditate, or pray. It is not that people do not care about such things, it is that time often equals achievement, success, or money. If a minute or an hour is lost, we feel guilty. I need to read and listen to what I am writing, because I often feel an anxiety attack if I am not working on something that seems productive. At best, that is pitiful, absolutely pitiful.

This sense of hurry does something to us. Does more than deplete our energy or make us weary. Hurriedness in life disqualifies us for the work of conversation and prayer which, alone, develops relationships that meet the most profound human need. There are heavy demands put upon our work, true; there is difficult work to be engaged in, yes. But the thoughtful Christian, if he or she is to serve others, need not appear "busy."

Busyness can be an illness of the spirit; a rush from one thing to another because there is no ballast of "life-integrity," and no confidence in the primacy of grace. In life there must be a wide margin of quiet leisure, which helps to define the ordinary, technological dehumanizing definitions that are imposed upon us by the society in which we pilgrimage.

Henri Nowen writes: "Without the solitude of heart, our relationships with others easily become needy and greedy, sticky and clinging, dependent and sentimental, exploitative and parasitic, because without the solitude of heart we cannot experience the others as different from ourselves but only as people who can be used for the fulfillment of our own, often hidden, needs."

Maybe that is why the Scriptures say, "Be still and know that I am God."

It's worth pondering.

# More Important than What God Is Called

A large number of people, both inside and outside the Church, are talking about appropriate words that describe the nature of God. Much of this talk has been sparked by newspaper reports about three prayers in the newly adopted *United Methodist Book of Worship.*

The new *Book of Worship* is not *law* for the Church. Its use by pastors, musicians, and lay people is voluntary, and it will not be in the pew racks of the congregation. Its primary purpose is to be a resource for those who plan worship for the many occasions in the life of any congregation. For example, there is a "Service For The Renewal Of Marriage Vows." I hope that some of our members will choose to use this service as an act of public worship on the occasion of a wedding anniversary. Services to fit almost every day and special situation are in the book. No one has to use them, but we can if we so choose.

In the *Book of Worship*, as in the Bible, God is referred to in many ways. Since the beginning of time people have used many images and metaphors to point to God. "Father" is the most used description, but it is by no means the only expression. Isaiah 66: 12–13, for example, sees mothering qualities in Jehovah. Other Old Testament words used for the God who cannot be fully explained are:

> El, which literally means God or Deity.
> El Shadday, which means God, the One of the Mountain.
> El Elyon, which means Exalted One, or Most High.
> El Olam, which means God, the Everlasting One, or God of Eternity.
> El Roi, perhaps means God, Who Sees Me.
> El Berith, which means God of the Covenant.
> El Israel, which literally means God of Israel.
> Elohim, which is perhaps translated Godhead.
> Eloah, which occurs forty-two times in the Book of Job and comes close to meaning the God of Israel.
> Adon, which is translated Lord.

God in the Old Testament is also referred to as a Rock, a King, a Judge, a Shepherd, and a Father.

In the New Testament Jesus is referred to as the Son of David, Son of God, the Good Shepherd, the Great Physician, Savior; King; the Stone; the Bread of Life; the Messiah; the Door; the Way, the Truth, and the Life; the Judge; the Lamb; the Light of the World; the High Priest; the Amen; the Alpha and the Omega; the Firstborn of All Creation; the Bright and Morning Star; the Lord; and the God.

The new *Book of Worship*, like the Bible uses many of these same images for God. All of these words help us to consider the notion that God is greater than any thought form that the human mind can put together.

There is, in my judgment, something more important than what we call God. The more crucial issue is whether or not we will listen to "the still small voice," and whether or not we will obey.

Both how we speak to God and how we listen to God are very important. It's worth pondering.

# Reeboks and a Real Friend

I do not see very well without my eyeglasses. I can discern most things, but I cannot read. Last week, I was attending a meeting in a distant city. On Tuesday morning I went out for a jog. I was well equipped with Reeboks, rainsuit, and a turtleneck sweater for warmth. Had everything I needed, except my eye wear. Made it fine until I stopped my run to go inside an open church.

Rarely have I been inside a church that spoke to me as did this one. It is located near the bank of the mighty Mississippi River, where one can almost feel the current's tug. The sanctuary had just been redecorated with soft blues and slightly contrasting white beams and woodwork. The chancel area points beyond itself to that which remains a mystery and is yet revealed.

Anyone who knows me understands that I have a compulsive love affair with reading. Almost every time I sit down I grab for something to read. And so it was that day.

As I sat in a pew for a time of prayer and reflection, I automatically reached for a booklet that was lying on the face of the hardwood pew. Picked it up, but I could not read it. Letters and words blurred together into one glob of a paragraph. I squinted, turned my head to-and-fro, and moved the page forward and back, but I could not make out even one complete sentence.

Since I could not read, I thought my thoughts, revalued my values, and went deep within myself. Time passed very quickly. My loved ones, events, people, and situations flooded my being. Right in the midst of all that cascaded through me, I experienced a sure sense of God's presence. The mystics would call it a transcendental experience. Some would say that it was like experiencing the Holy One. Whatever label you put on it, the experience was a genuine God-connection.

In that one fleeting moment I experienced God as a caring friend.

Some people see God as a wrathful judge. Some as a distant creator. Some as that than which nothing greater can be conceived. Some as love. Some as a strong father. Some as a nurturing mother. At times I have experienced God in all of these ways, and more. But on that Tuesday morning, I felt the friendship of God.

A true friend is one with whom we can unburden ourselves and know that we are going to be heard and accepted regardless of what we say or feel. A friend is one who instinctively accepts the otherwise unacceptable in us.

To consider God as one who is near and not far away is to think of God as being in everything, because all that is has the potential for being Holy.

Friendship is an unpretentious relationship, for *friend* is not a designation of office, nor an exalted title, nor a function one must perform from time to time, nor a role one is supposed to play in society. Friendship is personal. It combines both affection and respect. One neither looks up or down at a friend. One can look a friend in the face. In friendship, one experiences oneself just as one is, readily accepted and respected in one's own freedom.

In addition, friends are people who listen. And so, if we think of God as a friend, we will see God as one who cares enough to listen, to care, and to answer.

It's worth pondering.

# A Ground-level View

Recently I heard a woman say, "Everything that is worthwhile is dissolving around us." Though there is an element of truth in what she said, I would like to look at it another way. Could it be possible that in the midst of all the mess that God is working to create a new heaven and a new earth? If God is creating a new heaven and a new earth (Revelation 21), then we should join in and participate in what God is doing. Whatever happens to this world is a joint venture between God and ordinary people like you and me. This way of looking at things suggests openness to the spirit on the part of those of us who believe.

Is God at work in the advance of nonwhite people all around the globe? Is God at work in the emancipation of women? Is God at work in new and massive efforts to feed the children of the earth? How we answer those questions and many others depends largely upon our perspective. We all see it one way if we are locked into a ground-level view, as compared to looking at the world from God's perspective. From God's perspective, a new heaven and a new earth is being born. Unless we strain to see as God sees, we see only the chaos of the world.

I have the conviction that God wants us to be hooked into the new creation. Why we stay stubbornly locked into a ground-level view is worth pondering.

# Unannounced

One of my primary interests has been to help skeptics come to a living faith. As I prepare sermons or lessons, I am aware that there might be some person present who is sitting on the edge of belief. To enable that person to move from unbelief to belief is sometimes a short, but at other times a long journey. Most of the time we move toward Christianity by what C. S. Lewis called "joy" or "romance." Others have called it revelation. This refers to those fleeting experiences that almost everyone has had at one time or another. It refers to those moments when God's presence was real and certain.

These revealing moments may be triggered by a bar of music, a landscape, a note from a dear friend, or the surfacing of a forgotten memory.

This experience is an instantaneous sense of seeing into the heart of things. It was as though a reality beyond all reality opened itself wide for an instant and, just as instantly, slammed its doors shut. Mystics and poets such as Wordsworth have often written about such experiences. Milton called it the "enormous bliss" of Eden. Longfellow speaks of it in his "Saga of King Olaf."

Most of us, I think, go for long periods of time unvisited by such revelatory experiences. Then, in rather surprising ways, they come unannounced and in full strength. These fleeting revelations of God's presence continue off and on for most of our lives.

When I was about twelve years of age, I had such an experience while walking home from our neighborhood church. Except for the blinking of a few stars, the night was as dark as pure black. As I traveled toward home, a feeling of God's presence washed over me. I was not looking for it. It came unannounced.

It is worth pondering.

# Grace

# Being Somewhere

On December 30th, I joined various members of Janene's family by participating in a Golden Wedding anniversary given in honor of her parents, Leonard and Deloris Dunavant. It was a grand affair. A huge cloth-covered table was laden with tasty food, punch, and coffee. The center of the table held an oversized arrangement of yellow roses, flanked by an assortment of greenery. Yellow ribbons gave the table festive color. A three-layered cake was mounted on a decorative table, which was framed by a flowered arch. Tables with gold balloons were scattered here and there.

For two and a half hours people tramped in and out of that pretty room. Congratulations were offered. Food was partaken. Laughter reverberated from the walls. The community came together to express feelings of love and appreciation for two people who have meant more than can be measured.

Near the end of the reception, I noticed an older man sitting alone at a nearby table. He wore both a well-worn suit and a grey beard. Both his hair and his tie needed to be straightened. His plate was so full that I wondered why it did not break under the load. Later, I learned that he and hard times were on a first-name basis. Though he was not like most of the people who came, he felt at home in that crowd of well-wishers.

Upon seeing this stranger, I went over and introduced myself by saying, "My name is Joe Pennel. I married Janene, the Dunavant's oldest daughter. We are truly glad that you are here." Quicker than a New York minute, he replied, "I'm glad to be here. Everybody's got to be somewhere."

That old timer is exactly right. "Everybody's got to be somewhere." Where we are should be determined by understanding Whose we are.

It's worth pondering.

# Saying Everything without Speaking a Word

Her name is Sarah. My wife, Janene, can still remember that day twelve years ago when Sarah was a member of her first-grade class. It was Janene's first class at the University School of Nashville (USN).

Janene and Sarah have a lot in common. They go to the same school. Have many of the same friends. Know the same teachers. Both love basketball. And both have been at the University School for twelve years.

If you have read thus far, you know that Sarah is now in the spring of her senior year. It's an important year for Janene and Sarah. Sarah will soon be graduating from high school along with Janene's first, first-grade class.

For twelve long years Janene has taken a keen interest in each of "my first graders," as she continues to refer to them. She has watched them pass from grade to grade. She's been interested in their majors and minors, and noticed their boy friends and girl friends. She's kept up with where each one will be attending college. There is something special about this senior class, and that something spans twelve years of learning together.

The feel between Janene and her first graders is even more intense right now, because it is tournament time in prep basketball, and Sarah is a key player on the USN team. She is not the tallest, but she is the fastest. She is what they call "quick" . . . very quick. In a blink she can make a steal. She can shoot from the outside, or she can fearlessly drive the basket for a bucket, or a foul, or both. When she dribbles on a fast break, her hair bounces up and down like it's being blown by an oversized fan. She does not tire easily, and the closer the score, the more she seems to take charge. Intense is the word for it. Play hard, straight ahead, and no fooling around—that's Sarah.

When I go to a tournament game with Janene, I find myself watching my wife as well as the game. I have discovered that Janene watches all five players, but she has a special eye for Sarah. When Sarah makes a routine free shot she says, "Way to go, Sarah." When Sarah commits a foul she groans, "Oh, Sarah." And, when the referee makes a bad call on Sarah, I'll not say what she says. But, when Sarah makes a clutch shot, Janene jumps up out of her seat and shouts— I mean shouts—"That's my Sarah!"

In a unique way, Janene is involved in the game with Sarah. It's not because they visit very often, because they do not. It's not because our families know each other. It's not because Sarah turns to Janene for advice. Janene is involved in the game with Sarah because of a tie—a union which started the very day that those twenty-two six-year-olds walked into Janene's class. Though Janene no longer teaches first grade, there is a bond that will not be broken by human failure or the passing of time.

Maybe God loves us like Janene loves Sarah. When we score well, God probably shouts, "That's my Joe"—or whomever. When we foul out, God's forgiving and redeeming heart must go out to us. Sometimes, God loves us with a proud and happy heart, and ofttimes God loves us with a sad and broken heart, but it is the same love.

In a few weeks the graduation exercises will take place at the University School of Nashville. All of the king's horses and all of the king's men could not keep Janene away from the best seat in the house. I do not know how or where it will happen, but I expect that Janene will have a big lump in her throat when her first graders walk across the stage. And my prediction is that when the graduation activities are concluded and when the crowd is milling around, Janene and Sarah will find a way to hug each other.

It does not matter what they will say to each other, though a whisper should be shared between them. The hug, the tie, the bond—the future—that's what really matters.

"Way to go, Sarah!" "Way to go, Janene!"

Way to go every time we give ourselves to each other!

It's worth pondering.

# The Necessity of Saving and Changing

As a preacher of the gospel I bear a great responsibility for the souls of this congregation. This self understanding is not an idle thought; it turns my mental and spiritual energy like a tiny axle turning a mighty wheel.

I want the gospel that is preached in this congregation to both interpret life and to alter life. Interpreting life from the vantage point of the Christian faith is an important part of our task. But we must go further. We need to so proclaim the gospel that the character and ethos of life is altered.

There is always the danger of preaching the kind of grace that saves us without changing us. Emphasis on saving grace alone can serve as a palliative to our conscience, without changing the basic character of our lives. A gospel that does not change us does not require fairness toward others, nor does it call us to be more and more loving.

John Wesley, the founder of Methodism, would have nothing to do with the sort of grace that saves us without changing us. If that is the case, then how do we know that we are being changed? If divine love is actively working to restore the image of God in us, we are being changed. We know that we are being changed if we are growing in our imitation of God's love.

May all that is taught and learned in this congregation result not only in the interpretation of life, but also in the changing of life.

It is worth pondering.

# Lent, Holy Week, and Easter

# Busy Whittlin'

Back when I was a rural pastor, I enjoyed going "to town," as we called it. It was a scant fifteen miles from Enville to Henderson, which was our county seat. It was not a long drive, but it was a long way from our village of 200 people to our "going to town place." Henderson had things that Enville would never have. Things like a college, physician, high school, mom and pop stores, a couple of meat-and-three restaurants, a jail, and the courthouse.

The courthouse benches, both inside and out, were more often than not filled with men who either played checkers or whittled. The red and black squares on the checkerboard were almost erased from constant use. Since the regulation checkers had long since been lost or broken, bottle tops were faithfully called into service. Coke bottle tops served as red checkers while root beer tops acted as black checkers.

Pop Guin was the undisputed checker champion. Every now and then someone would slip up and beat him, but not often. And when someone did edge out Pop, it was big news all over town. Over the years Pop has become the best known character in the county. He knew how to play checkers, and he would take on anybody who was big enough to get up to the board.

The whittlers were also an interesting bunch. They came early and stayed late. Most always the same familiar faces. Most always the same pile of shavings, the same knives, the same people, and the same benches. A few of the men were known as "drivers." They drove their wives to work at the shirt factory and then drove them home in the afternoon, after having whittled and played checkers all day. My good friend, Travis, often observed that the whittlers whittled, but they "never made anything." He also said that the checker players were "entertaining themselves to death."

And that is a danger for all of us. Like those men at the courthouse, we are in danger of whittling away at life and not making anything. Life degenerates to nothing more than eating bland meals in restaurants, making the mortgage payments, working, waiting for the weekend, paying tuition, bills, giving enough away to salve our conscience, having two or three genuine friends, and being in bondage to the gods and pressures of our own making. It is easy to drift through life and not make anything. Not to be involved in some concern that will outlive us is a sad and terrible way to live.

There is also the danger of entertaining ourselves to death. I am saddened by the hoards of people who cannot be involved in worship, nurture, and outreach because they have given entertainment a top priority. Words often heard are, "I cannot come to worship because I have a tennis match," or "I cannot attend a committee meeting because that's my bridge night," or "We cannot be involved in a group for Bible study because our calendar is already full with soccer, golf, the theater, the club, our boat, or a favorite T.V. program."

Now, I am not putting down entertainment because it, like all things, has a place in our hardworking lives. But sometimes people are in danger of believing that the purpose of life is to have fun and be entertained.

Lent tells us that there is more to life than whittling and entertainment. It speaks to us about the abundant life that can come from following the way of Christ. Jesus, as we know from the New Testament, identified with the pains and pressures of people. He gave himself to God and for others. He has shown us that the ultimate joy comes from giving ourselves away.

As strange as it seems, we are not forced to look for opportunities to give ourselves to others. Such opportunities come every day. They meet us around every corner. Hurts and hopes come dressed in those very persons whose eyes and hearts are opened toward us.

The tragedy is that we might be so busy whittlin and searching for entertainment that we would miss experiencing Christ when he comes dressed in the garb of another person's need.

# The Rhythms of Life

S tir crazy. Those are two of the words that characterize much of our frenzied activity and life together. We are incredibly busy people. We move from thing to thing, person to person, task to task, mountain to mountain, opportunity to opportunity. We are driven, forsaken, ambitious, tireless, motivated, strung out. Yet, in the midst of all of this busyness, life lacks a certain rhythm.

There needs to be a time of "sabbath" in all our lives. A sabbath time, which is a time apart from the stir crazy side of life, should have four parts to it.

First, there should be a time for ceasing. This means that there should be a time for us to simply quit what we are doing, to stop, to draw the line, to refuse to do any more. When we cease for a while, we can usually go back to our tasks with more vigor, resourcefulness, and creativity.

In the second place, we need to see the value of resting. By resting we mean to relax, to let down inside, to get in touch with the rivers that run deep inside our souls. Resting is not easy for many of us because most of us are hyper, and we place a far greater value on working than we do on resting. Yet resting brings with it a certain amount of restoration, and this can bring its own gift.

Embracing is the third quality that is needed in any sabbath time. By embracing, I mean to lay hold of the tradition that has come to us. To take time apart to embrace those truths and values that have been given to us by the generations that have gone before us. For example, reading the Scripture, or classics, or a biography of a great person of the past, or merely to stop and reappropriate the heritage that comes to us over a period of time. If we do not embrace that which has gone before us, our lives can be rudderless, and we will unknowingly repeat in the present the mistakes of the past.

The fourth quality that a sabbath time needs is that of feasting. Feasting with family, friends, and significant others in our lives can bring a special joy. Sitting around the table, holding hands, telling stories, singing songs, can feed the spirit.

I understand that a survey was once done of distinguished people who had graduated from Harvard University. There were about fifty people in this survey. All fifty of these people had one thing in common. All of them shared feast times with their families, and all of them shared the evening meal with their parents and siblings. Feasting is about more than eating. It is about talking and listening, planning and dreaming, forgiving and loving.

In this stir crazy time we need more holy rhythms in our lives. Times when our spirits can be held, nurtured, and loved. Not only will these holy rhythms make us more compassionate, they will also make us be more courageous and more visionary.

We will soon be entering the season of Lent, a time of repentance and preparation for the crucifixion and resurrection of Jesus Christ. As we think about what we will "give up" for Lent, let us also think about "taking up" some holy rhythms that can bring restoration and direction to the stir craziness that all of us share.

It's worth pondering.

# Hope, Not a Wish

Easter has often been called the season of great hope. Gabriel Marcel has made it clear that what many people call hope is in fact a form of wish-fulfillment thinking. All of us know that the life of any person is filled with wishes.

A child wishes for a bicycle, a boy wishes for a football, a student wishes for a car, a house, a job. A sick person wishes to be cured; a poor man, to become rich; a prisoner, to become free.

This wish fulfillment thinking is like waiting for a Santa Claus, whose task it is to satisfy very specific needs and desires, if possible, immediately. When our lives are filled with this type of specific concrete wishes, we are in constant danger of becoming disappointed, bitter, angry, or indifferent, since some of our wishes do not come true. When that happens, we begin to feel that somewhere and somehow we have been betrayed.

Easter speaks to us about a different kind of hope. The hope of Easter is directed toward God who is able to bring life from death. At the resurrection, the community comes to life again, the scattered are reassembled, the disillusioned become full of faith, the frightened become fearless, and those who denied and deserted are forgiven. The hope of Easter is that some day time will be shot through with grace upon grace, and God's promises will shape creation's great conclusion.

Christian hope is, therefore, more than wish-fulfillment. We "wish that," but we "hope in."

That is the difference, and it is worth pondering.

# Life Is Big Time

ife is BIG TIME. The big time is not something that we get to some day. Not a destination. Not an arrival point. The big time is now. It is every precious minute of every passing day. This morning I walked out to our pebble-topped driveway to fetch the morning paper. As I made that short trip, I saw the dogwoods in full bloom, heard the song of birds, smelled the freshly cut grass, felt the soft breeze pushing against my face, and when I came back to the house I let orange juice roll across my tongue. In a scant few minutes I experienced a big slice of life. This is the big time.

The ancient Hebrews thought that we had to experience everything with our five senses. That is what I did this morning. I let all five senses wrap themselves around five sixty-second periods of the day. It was a joy, and it was not the minor leagues.

When we are open to life with our five senses, we begin to see life as a collection of extremities. On the one side there is terror, despair, catastrophes, tragic ruin, flood, famine, torture, and disease. On the other side there is nature in her every aspect, brutal or smiling, and a persistent smolder of kindness in the greater mass of humankind. There are stars and animals and trees and microbes; there are people to love and friends who are good, and all shapes and sizes of people who do the goofiest things imaginable. And, if you look for it, there is a lovely quiet in the midst of hilarious turmoil. There is the rational side of life, and the circus of sense and circumstances.

This life is the BIG TIME! Take up the yardstick of life and see if the extremities of horror and joy, despair and contentment, were not ends of the same standard and composed of the very same materials.

And, if we take away the stuff of tears, there is nothing left to make laughter of. How about that sentence?

I believe that life is the big time because I believe the message of Easter, which is that life is stronger than death.

It is worth pondering.

# Love Stronger than Death

The New Testament book of John depicts the cross as glorious. But what is so glorious about the cross of Christ? It is the central symbol of the Christian faith. It stands at the center of our worship. It is "processed" every Sunday morning near the beginning of the service. But why did John call it glorious?

In the world of Jesus it was a horrible form of death. It was reserved for insurrectionists and the dregs of society. When a writer said, "He was crucified," everyone knew what that meant. So, what is so glorious about Jesus experiencing that kind of death?

This question is best answered by considering the larger context. The bigger picture is the great struggle which took place between Jesus and the forces that were hostile to God. In the life of Jesus we see success and failure, popularity and enmity, joy and suffering, and conflicts with the spiritual and temporal powers. Throughout his earthly ministry He faced opposing forces.

When Jesus was put to death on the cross, it appeared that the opposition had won. It seemed that evil had nailed good to a tree. It gave some evidence that the "Herods" had silenced what God was doing in Jesus by making him the victim. It witnessed to the failure of Jesus' mission.

However, for Christians, the crucifixion is not the end of the story. Three days later God raised Jesus from the dead. In so doing, God said that the sacrificial love that was in Jesus could not be defeated by the power of evil. In raising Jesus, God said that love is stronger than death and that good had triumphed over evil. The battle with the powers of evil had been fought, and won! The victim had been made the victor.

In some parts of the world people make kites and fly balloons on Good Friday. Such celebration takes place not because of a man who hung on a cross, but because of how God brought victory from what seemed to be defeat.

We will gather Sunday to witness to our belief in the resurrection. We will gather as an Easter people—people who believe that Christ lives and has not been defeated.

May those who do not believe this central claim of the Christian faith wish that they could.

It is worth pondering.

# Giving Up to Take Up

I have been taught that one should give up something for Lent. Giving up something is a way of practicing self-denial, which is a constant reminder that Jesus gave himself for us. Doing without is no virtue in and of itself. We can give up almost anything and remain more and more like we have always been. However, if we give up something as a method for reminding ourselves of our Lord's passion, that act of giving up can become a helpful spiritual discipline.

But, there is another side to the proverbial coin—a side that is not often mentioned. The other side is to also take up something for Lent, as a way of reminding ourselves that Christ took up the cross of love for us. One could take up being ethical in all relationships, being regularly involved in outreach, speaking out for justice and against injustice, prayerfully caring for one's body, reading and studying the Scripture each day, praying privately each day, attending worship every Sunday (unless prevented), obeying the prompting of the Holy Spirit, or being intentionally involved in advancing the cause of Christ.

How all of life involves both giving up and taking up is worth pondering.

# The Pain of Loving and Not Loving

I like to go to the movies on cold, rainy Saturday afternoons; those afternoons when I cannot be outside for either work or pleasure. While at the theater, I am transported into another world. Watching a good show is like reading a good book. I get caught up in it and I identify with either the plot or one of the principal characters, or sometimes both.

When it is a strong and wonderful movie, I like to stay to read the credits. I have never said that to anyone, because I have always felt that the person or persons that I am with would often prefer to leave at the conclusion of the last line. But I would prefer to read that long list of credits, because I have this strange desire to know the people behind the characters.

Maybe I want to read the credits because I have always had this buried desire to be on stage. Acting would provide me the opportunity to present myself as many different persons. Through acting, I could be that which real life will never provide.

When I was in high school, I got a taste of what the stage would feel like. I landed a part in the senior play. Thought it would be a piece of cake, until I started learning my lines. At the early rehearsals our drama coach would say over and over, "Learn your lines. You have got to learn your lines." I soon found out that the first step toward an effective play was for every actor and actress to know the lines. It was impossible to move into character without the lines having been committed to memory.

In a very real sense, Holy Week is a time for Christians to "learn the lines." It is here that we reread and relearn the Passion Story. In relearning these lines we come face-to-face with One who chose His pain.

That is the choice that is before each of us. We, like Jesus, can choose our pain. Jesus chose the way of love and it brought vulnerability and suffering. I do not know anyone who can deny that when we set out to love another person, we open ourselves to the possibility of suffering. Love is getting close and establishing intimacy with others, and this makes for vulnerability. But having said that, does it automatically follow that by not loving one is assured of not having to suffer?

There is a form of pain that goes with love, and there is a kind of pain that goes with not loving. Joseph Gallagher is right on target in saying, "Our human choice is never between pain and no pain, but between the pain of loving and not loving." Pain is an inevitable part of life, no matter how hard we try to live it, or which way we attempt to go. Therefore, it is futile to try to escape pain completely.

There is no desire embedded any deeper in our makeup than the desire not to suffer; yet this becomes a tragic illusion if we elevate it to a life goal. There is pain involved no matter which way we turn, so the quicker we disabuse ourselves of this fantasy that we can avoid suffering altogether, the better. If we refuse to do this, we will only bring greater and greater suffering into our lives, for our very attempts not to suffer will lead us farther and farther from reality.

*Mr. and Mrs. Bridge* is a very good movie. I saw it last week on a cold, rainy afternoon. It is about the pain that comes when we choose not to love. Holy Week is about the pain that comes when the way of love is selected. The pain of *Mr. and Mrs. Bridge* leads to separation and death. The passion of Christ leads to life.

When we get our lines straight, we understand that to be true.

It's worth pondering.

# Paying Attention

P aying attention is hard work. "Pay attention" are words that have often pounded my eardrum. Heard it from my mother. My teachers. My wife. My children. The person sitting across the desk. Heard it all of my "live long" life.

Since I make speeches and write things, it is important that I pay attention to the ebb and flow of life. Being a keen observer is one of the prerequisites for those of us who comment on life from the vantage point of the Christian religion.

Seeing what happens in the course of a typical day can provide great enjoyment. It is fun to watch the drama of everyday life.

Look at that person sitting at a table across the restaurant. He is wearing a neat sport shirt, pressed jeans, and an old paint cap which is spotted with every color in the rainbow. His shoes are clean and shined to a high gloss. Why is his hat so out of character with the rest of his clothing? Is his hat the best that he has? Or is it a practical joke? Does it reflect a sense of honor? Is he trying to make a statement? Why does he not take it off while eating in public? Is it a good luck piece? Perhaps a way of getting recognition? I watched that man with the funny cap for about sixty seconds, and he provided me one full minute of pure fun.

Not only can the observance of everyday life bring pure joy, it can also be charged with the mystery of providential care. When seen in this way, life can be filled with the "Holy," even when it is fragmentary, fragile, and ambiguous. If we look carefully we will begin to see divine clues in human experience.

It is important that we pay attention to those everyday experiences that might contain some hint of the holy. Pay attention to the unexpected sound of your name on somebody's lips. The good dream. The strange coincidence. The moment that brings tears to your eyes. The person who brings life to your life. Even the smallest events hold the biggest clues.

Luke's account of the resurrection is like an event that happened along the way. On the day of the resurrection, two men were walking to a village named Emmaus. As they walked along the road, Jesus himself drew near and went with them. Luke says that the eyes of these two men were kept from recognizing him. In a word, the risen Christ appeared to them, but they did not see Him.

My word to you this Easter is very simple. It is that the risen Christ appears to us each and every day. He is around every corner. He is in the people we meet, the things we see, the experiences that we have. He comes to us, comes to us, and comes to us.

It is in the everyday experiences that we will meet Him. The everyday experiences of people, Bible reading, praying, listening, and seeing.

Why we do not see Him when He comes is worth pondering.

Pay attention.

# Reece's Timing

Reece is a neat little fellow. He is three years old and he's full of life. Recently, Reece's mother could not find a sitter so she brought him with her to a meeting of the congregation's Finance Committee. Reece entered the room with paper, crayons, and a soft drink tucked under both of his tiny arms.

Julian Cornett, who chairs the Finance Committee, called the meeting to order. I offered a prayer. Folders were passed to each member of the committee. The committee then started reviewing the receipts and disbursements for

1989. While business was being transacted, Reece was as restless as a one-legged frog on the expressway. Every few minutes, Reece would pause from his coloring, drinking, and drawing to listen to "adult talk."

About ten minutes into the meeting, I saw Reece tugging at his mother's dress. After capturing his mother's attention, Reece spoke loudly enough for all to hear, "Mother, is it time to sing? When are we going to sing?" "We do not sing at a Finance Committee," whispered his mother. As laughter filled the room, Reece piped up and said, "We always sing in the big church."

For the past couple of months Reece has been attending the 8:30 worship service. His powers of observation must be strong because he has noticed that the offering plates are always presented to the Reverend Donald R. Choate, who in turn offers the Prayer of Dedication and places them on the communion table. Reece pulled at his mother's dress, got her attention, and inquired, "When are they going to pass the bowls so they can be given to God?" I expect that Don Choate has been called by many names, but I have absolutely no doubt that Reece is the only one to call him "God."

The words of Reece are both right and wrong. He is wrong about singing in the Finance Committee, passing bowls, and about Don Choate being God. But, he is right on target in understanding that special things are supposed to happen at certain times.

Next week is one of those special weeks when certain things are to happen. Next week is Holy Week. It focuses on the passion of our Lord as lived out in the last days of His life. His entry into Jerusalem, the Lord's Supper, the crucifixion, are the days which are to be faithfully observed by devoted Christians. Observance of these days will enable us to be prepared to experience and bear witness to the resurrection of Christ. Everyone who follows Christ should make careful plans to follow Him through the observance of Holy Week.

For many persons, next week is just another week, or spring break, or business as usual. Many in our culture see Easter as just another holiday. But for Believers, next week is not just another week. It is a week made holy by what God did for all humanity through the sacrificial love of Christ. Therefore, it is the most important week in the Christian year.

It's worth pondering.

# What Love Does

Lent, like no other time of the year, is a time to observe the passion, death, and resurrection of Jesus—a time of penitence, prayer, and fasting. It is a time to seriously examine our life in the light of His life. And that is the rub, because most of us readily acknowledge that there is a radical incongruity between Christ's chosen way of life, as we are reminded of it in the Scripture, and the lives that so many of us live today— so secure, easy, protected, if not downright extravagant and self-enhancing.

Christ's lifestyle was vastly different from ours. That difference was vividly pointed out by a poor, but devout woman who lived in a shack located on a hillside outside of Rio. She said, "Can you imagine Jesus Christ living in one of those buildings in Copacabana or Ipanema (where the rich of Rio live)? Can you imagine Him boasting that He owns many cars and boats, has lots of money in the bank, and owns a big house on the ocean, south of Rio, besides His apartment here? I clean for them, the big shots, I know how much they own. There is only one piece of property they don't own: heaven! They can't buy it even with the millions and millions of cruzeiros [Brazil's monetary unit] you hear them mentioning all the time. God came to us as a poor man, the nuns say, and that must mean a lot! I tell my children that they would live better if they'd been born luckier, born to a Copacabana businessman. But that is one life. There are two lives we have to think about: this life and another life to come."

More often than I would like to admit, I, as one of the world's rich people, question how far I ought to follow the example of Christ. How far should I pursue humility, generosity, compassion, and self-sacrifice? The culture tries desperately to squeeze me into another mold. It tries to convince me that self-importance, self-cultivation, and eager pursuit are the hallmark of a successful person.

So what is God's Word to those of us who know not what it is to have not? What is God's Word to those of us who do not know the poor and the marginalized of the world? Is there a word for those of us who stand at a distance as if to thank God that "we" are not like "them"?

One of the hallmarks of the well-educated, well-off people is to claim our innocence. We can find a plethora of ways to get ourselves off the hook. We are professional at rationalizing our lack of responsibility for the poor, the broken, and the misguided.

What, then, is God's Word to the wealthy of the world? I say that those of us who live in Brentwood are wealthy when compared to most of God's children. Fully ninety-five percent of all the people in God's creation have less . . . far less.

Strangely, however, Christ has the same word for the rich and for the poor. Christ's Word is simple, direct, and to the point. Christ's Word will not be misunderstood. It is "love one another." Herein lies the answer. There is no greater power for the solving of the world's ills than genuine, selfless love.

Love feeds the hungry and clothes the poor. Love heals. Love gives leadership to the lost. Love makes it possible for enemies to become friends, wars to cease, and peace to reign. Love reaches out without qualification and strengthens the weakened soul. Love never loses its power nor does it lose hope. Love sees the dignity in all human beings. Love enables us to share, and sharing is the answer to most of the problems that we bring upon ourselves.

It's worth pondering.

# The Continuing Easter

In the secular world, Easter is a day. In the Church, Easter is a season that goes from Easter-day to Pentecost. Easter is more than the celebration of springtime. More than a secular holiday. More than ceremonial family gatherings. More than the vague belief that teachings of Jesus will live forever like the plays of Shakespeare. More than the elusive notion that the spirit of Jesus is undying, like that of Socrates. More than the humanistic belief that the spirit of Jesus lives in all who follow His earthly example.

Easter is not about something that we do. It is about that which God has done and continues to do. It is about a God who will not be stopped in efforts to redeem the world.

However, if we read the morning papers, it does not look like redemption is taking place. It looks as if pain and destruction are on the rise. Looks like the principalities and powers are entrenched. Looks like more and more people live under law than under grace. Looks like society has cracked. Looks like everything that was once nailed down is now coming up.

The Easter people, however, know that things are different. People of faith believe that the powers of this world are not as they seem. We believe that in spite of signs to the contrary, God's continuing work of redemption will not be stopped. We believe that the God of the empty tomb cannot be contained.

If the resurrection of Jesus is true (and I believe it to be so), then we must affirm the belief that the God of redemption will finally win. Ultimately, God will win over evil. Love will win over hate. Right will win over wrong.

Several years ago, Gloria Dick, the organist of old St. John's Church, came down with a life threatening illness. Her last trip out of the house was to go to the organ bench at St. John's. There, on a lonely afternoon with shadows drifting through the stained glass, her diseased fingers moved for the last time across the keyboard. With her back as straight as an arrow, and her head tilted back, she played "Christ the Lord Is Risen Today."

If you do not believe that God continues to redeem, tell the Gloria Dicks of the world. Convince her and all who so believe. Tell them that God's work was finished with the cross. Tell them that there is no such thing as the resurrection.

So, in this Eastertide, let those who believe join God in the continuing work of redemption.

Where we do that and how we do that is very important!

It is worth pondering.

# The Message of Easter

People who receive a good liberal arts education are challenged to ask "why?" "Why" is put to questions large and small. It is put to almost every phase of life. Why, for example, do people stand for the bride and not for the groom? Why do we pay some baseball players seven million dollars, while we cannot find money to build ball fields for the children of poverty? Why do we have ethics committees in business and government, when just being honest is all that is needed? Why do we take into our bodies food and drink that will cut short our life span? Why do we affirm belief in God, but spend so little time listening to what the Holy One is doing in our lives? Why do we miss so much of daily life, merely because we do not observe the beauty and holiness of every living minute?

Why do we talk about keeping the spirit of Christmas every day of the year, while we never say a word about keeping Easter all year long? It is like the meaning of Christmas should be kept, while the Easter message should be confined to one day.

Keeping the message of Easter is more important than trying to hold onto the Christmas spirit. I hold to this notion because Christmas is about birth, while Easter is about eternal love, which cannot be defeated by death. Death, as illustrated in the cross, does not have the last word! When God raised Jesus to be His Christ, God broke the power of death. So the big word of Easter is that love cannot be overcome.

Thus, the theological notion that Christ lives is of a greater consequence than the time and circumstances of his birth. I believe this to be true, because Jesus could have been born and not been raised. If he had not been raised, of what value would have been his birth?

Perhaps we do not talk about keeping the message of Easter all year because we know more about birth than continuing life. Who knows?

Anyway, it is worth pondering.

# What about Elvis?

I grew up in the same end of town as did Elvis Presley. I went to Treadwell and he went to Humes. I was a Methodist and he belonged to the Assembly of God church. I liked debate and he enjoyed the guitar. Other than that, we did not have much in common.

My earliest memory of Elvis took place at a softball field located in North Memphis. While my team was sweating out a ballgame, Elvis was sitting in the bleachers strumming a guitar. No one, except a few girls, paid any attention to Elvis. My teammates made fun of him. Called him a "sissy." Mocked his crooning voice. Dared him to get dirty with the rest of us.

My last memory of Elvis was at Baptist Memorial Hospital in 1976. I was visiting one of my parishioners who happened to be on the same floor. While attending to the member of my congregation, a nurse came into the room. I asked if she were the nurse for Elvis. Said she was. "How is he?" I inquired. With a voice soft as a slow rain, she replied, "Not good, not good at all. But have you heard that he gave me a new car?" Pointing to the keys pinned to her uniform she said, "Carry these with me all of the time. Would not let them out of my sight. He let me pick out the car that I wanted. It's a honey."

The recent decision of the United States Postal Service to create an Elvis Presley commemorative stamp has kicked up those youthful memories. Colonel Tom Parker would be proud that his boy from Third Avenue Public Housing Project had made it all the way to a stamp.

But which Elvis will grace the twenty-nine cent stamp: the young, fresh, Delta crooner of the hound-dog 1950s, or the more tragic, reclusive, middle-aged Las Vegas king who lay in the hospital bed down the hall?

The real tragedy about Elvis is that he was more of an image than a person. The person that I knew was shy. He had a ton of raw talent which stood ready to be packaged for the mainstream. He came along at a time when Madison Avenue was beginning to experiment with the new technology of mass communication, which was gearing up to give America a steady diet of new images, products, music, movies, and values. I have often wondered if it was timing that created the Elvis image, or if it was "the King" who pushed the new technology toward new vistas? Perhaps it was a combination of both. As debatable as that notion, Elvis will be remembered as a vitalizer of rock "n" roll, who created a unique blend of white country-and-western and black rhythm-and-blues. No one would dispute that.

But, which Elvis should be on the stamp? The image of Colonel Tom Parker's dream, or the tragic person who handled the enormous pressure to "be Elvis" by resorting to pills and booze?

Thinking about my sandlot friend and what became of his life has caused me to consider my journey. Am I more image or person? Lent gives me forty days, excluding Sundays, to measure the hidden and revealed places of my life.

Lent encourages me to look at myself, not for how I want "my public" to see me, but at what I need to see about myself.

Elvis and I have something in common. We are both marked by sin and grace, law and gospel, fear and hope.

No one will ever consider putting me on a twenty-nine cent stamp. But, I know beyond doubt that *I have been stamped* with the image of God. So have you. So has Elvis.

It's worth pondering.

# Sinners Redeemed

L ent, more than any time in the Church year, brings us face to face with our sinfulness. It is difficult for some of us to think of ourselves as sinners, because we associate "sinners" with what Dickens called the "dens of iniquity." However, Paul boldly said that "all of us have sinned and fallen short of the glory of God." Thus, none of us are spared the taint of sin, because all of us have tried to assert our own will against God.

Sin has such a hold on us that we do not have the power to break out of sin by our own actions or through our resolutions or decisions. Sin is always there before us, and it is vast and inescapable. We cannot run away from it or hide from it or deny it.

If we compare ourselves to others, we can feel virtuous, even proud. By comparison, we are no better and no worse than our neighbors. Such comparisons tend to help us deny our sinful natures. However, there is another comparison that is larger and more important.

During Lent, we compare ourselves not to our neighbors, but to what Christ achieved through His journey to the cross. When we compare ourselves to what was achieved through Christ, all of us are sinners because all of us fall short.

To put the matter rather bluntly: we sin each time we fail to live in the full-ness of Christ. If sin is falling short of the image of God that was in Jesus, then all of us are sinners. That, in my judgment, is what Paul meant when he said that "all have fallen short."

If Lent helps us to see ourselves as sinners, Easter points to how it is that we are redeemed from the sin that enslaves.

It is worth pondering.

# Life Lessons

# Little Decisions

The first little decision that I make each day is whether to go inside the Burger King or to use the "drive-thru." As I edge my vehicle past the yellow and red sign, I look to see how many cars are in line. If the automobiles are not backed up to the "order box," I will usually gamble by getting into the car lane. If the car line seems long, I will peer through the floor-to-ceiling plate glass window in order to catch a glimpse of how many biscuit eaters are standing in line. It is not an easy decision, because one never knows which line will move faster.

When I go inside to place my order, I always notice the last car in line, and when I depart with my large coffee and two creams, I check to see if I have beaten the last car.

Life is made up of a long list of little decisions like which line, what to eat, what to wear, and where to go. Every now and then life gives us the opportunity to make a large and pivotal decision, like how shall we participate in constructing new facilities which can serve God's children for years to come.

Little decisions are like sand in the shoes. Big decisions are similar to the mountains that we climb. Both are important, but some are more far-reaching than others.

It's worth pondering.

P.S. On most days the outside line is faster.

# A Full Barn or an Abundant Life

Since moving to our new home, Janene has decided to refinish an old chair. It is not an easy task, because each generation has covered one coat of paint with a coat of a different color. A combination of sandpaper, rags, steel wool, liquid stripper, and a ton of elbow grease has yet to remove all of the heavily sealed paint. The strongest bonding glue that ever came from Elmer's factory could not have a tighter bond. For days, Janene has been labor intensive about that old chair.

It is not a fancy chair. Quite the opposite. It is a rather plain rocker with a cane bottom and no arms. The back is slightly curved for an easy fit. It sits rather low, thereby making it more appropriate for a person with short legs. It was not made for watching TV, or reading, or for "couch potatoes." It will not recline in ten different positions. It's not overstuffed. Nor does it have any stuffing whatsoever.

If we tried to sell this "frontier-type" rocker at a yard sale, it would bring $10 or less. However, Janene would not take twenty times that much. She has developed a strong attachment to that one piece of furniture, not because of its market value, but because of the one for whom it was purchased. This chair is significant, because it belonged to Janene's Grandmother Dunavant, who used it to rock her young children.

Maybe the chair would not mean so much if Grandmother Dunavant had not been such a good woman. From the Dunavant oral tradition, I have learned that Grandmother Dunavant practiced the truth that the more you give away in love, the more you are. According to the standards of this world, Grandmother Dunavant never had much, but she was rich. She did not have a full barn, but she had an abundant life.

It's worth pondering.

# A Plain White Shirt

Most every Christmas someone will give me a new white dress shirt, with a button-down collar. My family thinks it rather ordinary that I should ask for the "same old-same old" each and every year. Perhaps they are right. But, receiving a new pinpoint white shirt is special for me.

There is a certain aura about a plain white shirt. It is clean and almost pure looking. No tears. No spots. No soiled places. No ring around the collar. No worn places from too much wear. No holes in the elbow. Every button is in place. It has a soft, pliable feel that will soon vanish with washing and starching. It provides a positive background for suit and tie.

I am not a user of dress shirts with many colors. Blue or white buttondowns will suit me just fine. I have some yellow and grey dress shirts that rarely get the privilege of being on my back. In and of themselves they are pretty, but they do not seem to fit what I have to put with them. When I do venture to wear one, I feel like I am on a display rack, or that I am dressed for the circus.

There is something about the white shirt that is more standard, more orthodox, more the way life is meant to be. They were acceptable yesterday. They are appropriate today. They will be just right for tomorrow.

My acceptance of the traditional white button-down probably says something about my conservative nature. I have never been quite certain about what a conservative is. That is because conservatives come in many shades and colors.

For me, a conservative is one who wants to "conserve" and pass on the best values and the higher righteousness of days gone by. Perhaps that is why the older I get, the more I am interested in the wisdom of old stories. My interest in "conserving" has drawn me back to the ancient tales of Moses, Abraham, Samuel, Jacob, David, Jesus, Paul, Peter, Calvin, Luther, Wesley, etc. I return to those told and retold stories with the desperate hope that I might hear a true and revealing word that would provide guidance for the mess we are in today. I have found that the lessons that one finds in the old stories have authenticity and grounding that one does not find in the new tales which arise out of situational ethics and conventional normality.

My recent reading and reflection have led me to the conclusion that the lessons from our distant past will better serve us in the present and in the days to come. The human family will get along much better, if we will heed the teachings of our past, which tell us to treat one another with "compassion, kindness, humility, gentleness, patience, forgiveness, and love." (Colossians 2:12–15)

Furthermore, the old conservative teaching from St. Paul beckons us to let love bind everything together, and to let the peace of Christ be the arbiter in our hearts. Guidance for our torn and troubled generation might better come from ancient insight and understandings of what constitutes real life.

Why we, as a global family, have not learned from the lessons of the past is worth pondering.

P.S. From time to time I jack up my courage and put on a blue button-down dress shirt, but never on Sunday!

# Catfish, Cornbread, and Christianity

He stood alone on the tee box. He was tall, muscular, bearded, and somewhat awkward. "Bud," I said, "is he playing solo?" Bud nodded and then invited the stranger to play the next nine holes of golf with us. As we played, I learned he was from Ohio and was going to graduate school on the GI Bill. So friendly was this chap that I decided to tease him.

After about five holes I said, "If you stay in Nashville long enough, we'll teach you to eat black-eyed peas, grits, cornbread, and catfish." "I like German food," he responded, with some emphasis on German. So abrupt was his retort that I carefully put the dietary habits of Southerners on the back-burner. As he walked the fairway to the last green, he coasted over to me and asked in a church whisper, "Do you really eat catfish?" I nodded in the affirmative. "Really?" Again, I motioned in the positive, growing curious at his insistence. "How could you?" he exclaimed. "Back home we throw them back or feed them to the cats."

Our regional food preferences are but one small indication of the differences that exist among people. We are not different altogether by choice, but are so because our backgrounds and cultures have molded us to see life differently; hold various views, cling to divergent political philosophies, practice certain customs, and accept different images of God. We notice our differences in the global village, throughout our neighborhood, and around our family dinner table. We can no longer afford to run from these differences, fight them, or ignore them. They need to be understood so that we can be in touch with one another.

Christianity proclaims that God came in Christ to transcend our differences and thereby make us one. Christ came not to make us carbon copies of one another, but to bring us compassionately together.

It's worth pondering.

# Life's Narthex and Chancel

Three times every Sunday morning I take a walk. After I give the "Sending Forth," I walk from the chancel to the narthex. It is a short walk. But it can be an exceedingly painful walk. Inside the chancel, rail life is ordered and poised. Hours and hours of preparation have gone into making what happens full of warmth and dignity, so that God can be worshiped.

It is here that the Scriptures are opened and the Word proclaimed. The plain old story is told and retold. Actions at the Table and Font set forth God's grace and providence. The choir leads the gathered voices of the people in the singing of hymns, the saying of prayers, and the recitation of the historic Psalms. For one precious hour each week, all truth is proportioned, contemporary, and complete. God's Word is proclaimed, affirmed, and responded to in ways that cannot be put into words.

But after fifty minutes have passed (never more because some clock watcher might get the hives), I lift my arms in benediction, which promises the blessing of God through the week that is yet to come. Then, I go to the narthex to greet the people as they leave the sanctuary to be Christ's people in today's world. Within fifteen minutes of the 11:00 AM service, the sanctuary is clear and the parking lot is all but empty.

In the chancel I work in an atmosphere of acknowledged faith and practice. Every detail is clear. All is carefully arranged under the sign of redemption. The wind of the spirit blows freely. Life is supported by the tradition of the Church. Living is reflected upon from the tradition of the Christian faith.

But in the narthex life is different. Those who have worshipped now make a disorderly reentry into the world of muddled marriages, midlife boredom, adolescent confusion, ethical ambiguity, and emotional stress. In the narthex I do not hold the cup of the Lord's Supper. I shake the hand of the man whose wife has left him for another. In the narthex I do not hold the infant for the waters of baptism, but I look into the eyes of a mother whose teenaged daughter is full of rebellion. The hands that just held the Scriptures now touch the hands of those who are tense with anxiety and fear. In the narthex I see veiled pain, an adulterer's secret, and an alcoholic's defeat.

As I stand in the narthex, I know that in the days that lie ahead there will be deaths no one expected, accidents no one thought possible, illnesses that defy diagnosis, and conflicts no one anticipated. But I also know that in the days that lie ahead there will be joy, peace, and many, many blessings yet untold and yet to be experienced. The narthex, like life, is a mixture of good and evil, pain and pleasure, joy and sorrow.

I often wonder what the narthex of life would be like without what happens in the chancel.

It's worth pondering!

# Nihilism and Despair

I have been reading "An Inner City Diary," which has been written by Brad Schmitt and Susan Thomas for *The Tennessean*. These articles are taken from the thirty day journal of these two reporters who lived incognito in East Nashville.

Reading these articles has reminded me of the congregation that I served in the late sixties that was located one street over from the largest housing project in the state of Tennessee. Like Brad Schmitt and Susan Thomas, I saw the despair, loneliness, and alienation of the people who existed and struggled in Hurt Village, which is the Memphis version of the James A. Cayce Homes.

While serving as a pastor in Hurt Village, I saw that the symbols for success were the kind of car that was driven, the kind of clothes that were worn, the kind of ornate (though often fake) jewelry that was bodily displayed, and the hair styles that made one fit in with the prevailing culture. In that sense, both the poor and the rich are united in a materialistic idolatry.

Here is the point: some of the problems that I saw in the ghetto life were vivid and frightening, but they have their parallels, less documented by journalism, in wealthy communities—drugs, craven materialism, insensitivity to others, and little moral tradition that seems to have any credibility for the people.

I have found nihilism and despair in both the poor ghetto and the wealthy suburb. Both the upper and the lower classes can serve the gods of materialism, and both are wrong in doing so. Both raw want and the curse of overabundance can push people toward immoral and unethical living.

It is worth pondering.

# Registered by Sin

I am forever mystified that some people seem to get results, while others get consequences. Those who get results seem to know how to live; they seem to connect with the grain of the universe. Reality works through them. The results come from harmonious, happy, effective living.

Other people seem to live only with consequences. No harmony. Unhappy. Ineffective. Always swimming against the stream. Forever working against the grain of the universe. Bucking the system. At every turn facing the consequences.

Two kinds of people are evident here. Some cooperate with the way God intends life to be and the results are self-evident.

A wise man once said that we do not break God's law, we break against it. Those who break against God's intentions are those who suffer the consequences of life.

E. Stanley Jones told about a woman who said, "It's all right to do these things [meaning acts of immorality] providing you get away with it." But, as I understand it, no one gets away with it. Maybe no one will ever find out, but the results will register in us, and we will have to live with ourselves.

My home church reared me on the passage, "Be sure your sin will find you out." While growing up I thought that passage meant, "Be sure your sin will be found out." But the Bible does not say that. It says, "Your sin will find you out"—will register in you, cause deterioration, decay; you will get a good dose of consequences in yourself.

Those who suffer the consequences of life are often those who try to manipulate life. Those who get results are those who try to find out what life demands and then work to fulfill those demands. This is not easy. In fact, it is a long and humbling experience.

Listen to it again. We must not try to manipulate life. Yet, I see many people who are trying to do just that—trying to make life work their way. In so doing they place themselves, and not life, at the center.

It is much easier to demand of life instead of listening to what life needs from us. The results of such seeking are written in frustration and wreckage.

If we are not humble toward life, we will be humbled.

The first step toward a useful, purposeful life is to be humble, to be teachable. To cease struggling and fighting and listen. If we are to find out what life demands of us, we must first listen to the One who has no voice.

How we do that is worth pondering.

# The Larger Questions

Igh school graduations are just over the fence. In a few days seniors will be walking across the stage, hearing their names called, receiving a diploma, and they will be given a big handshake by some representative from the school. In a scant few seconds their lives will turn toward a new tomorrow. Life will never be the same again. A shift will take place.

As this transition is taking place, some of the adults who are present for the graduation ceremonies will be reflecting on big questions.

"Are these graduates spoiled and self-indulgent, or will they be guided by compassion, respect, love, and willingness to be useful and helpful?"

"Has the faith been passed on to them so that they will know the value of spiritual and moral discipline?"

"Have they been trained by home and church to look at life as God sees it?"

"Will they become isolated from parents, aunts, uncles, cousins, grandparents, and the community wherein they were nurtured?"

"Will they choose a vocation where they can use their gifts and chase their God-given interests, or will they be claimed by a job that has no meaning, and about which there is not excitement?"

These questions—the questions that pound our minds on graduation day—will only be answered in the tomorrows of life. It is sobering to know that some of the seniors will not care about these larger questions. Others will give them passing thought and will decide not to answer. And some of our seniors will spend their entire lives trying to give an adequate and honorable answer to the bedrock and most important concerns of life.

I pray that a larger percentage of the seniors will be in the latter and not the former categories.

It is worth pondering.

# What to Ponder

S ome people will call it "daydreaming." I call it "pondering." With daydreaming the mind flits and wanders to this and that. With pondering the mind reflects with some intentionality on a given subject or line of thought.

I ponder all kinds of questions and situations. Questions like, "What's the purpose of the Church?" I suppose that I should have settled that one in my second semester of seminary. But it keeps hanging out there as a question that is not exhausted by any answer. Those who have listened closely to me know that I believe that the fundamental purpose of the Church is to continue the work of Christ on earth. In addition, I would like to see the Church as a moral and ethical community wherein Christian character is formed. I would like to see the Church model the life that was in Christ. I know that sounds rather high-flown, but it's the stuff that I ponder.

I also worry about what books and central teachings a modern day Christian should know, and how the congregation can serve the larger social good. I worry about what I am saying in sermons and what we are teaching in Sunday School. I worry about such things because I feel that we should be communicating the absolute essentials of our faith. If we, as the local congregation, do not clearly articulate the centrality of the Christian message, no one else will. It's our responsibility, and we must, for the sake of Christ and His people, accept the task.

We are so engaged in the practical, utilitarian life of power and consequence that we fail to see the Church as a sheltered space for deeply reflective moments—moments that can provide direction and purpose for the living of our days. We need a break from the fast-paced, banal existence that most of us endure every day. The local church, unlike any other collection of people, should provide that place, away from all other places, so that we might see more clearly the meaning of love. The Church should not always be the place where we come for more "activity," though activities are integral to our life together. If more activities are all that we have to offer, we might fail to offer a place to study, learn, reflect, worship, and "be."

I also ponder the virtues that we teach. I ask silly questions like, "Are we centering our teachings on the virtues of a competitive, acquisitive society, or are we drilling in those time-honored Christian virtues like humility, gratitude, wisdom, temperance, patience, forgiveness, and compassion?"

For the Church to speak to the real needs of real people is important to me. It's important that we engage life from the vantage point of the Christian faith. It's important that we are well grounded in our understanding of and commitment to the Gospel of Jesus Christ. To be supremely concerned about that which is central to our life together, as it relates to our understanding of who God is and what God expects of us, is of ultimate concern to me.

Many of the things that I ponder come to fruition every single day in the life and thought of this congregation. For that, all of us are most grateful.

A friend recently said, "Joe, how is the economy going to affect the congregation's income this year?" "Not at all," I replied, "because United Methodist Believers have a habit of tending to those things that are central to all and everything."

How we care for that which is central to the Church's mission is worth pondering.

# Life's Meaning

Today, many people suffer from a kind of meaninglessness that leads to separation, alienation, and despair from families, work, government, basic beliefs, themselves, and God. I hold to the notion that many of today's disorders are rooted in lack of meaning: drug abuse, alcoholism, sexual abuse, suicide, crime, broken relationships, moral failures, and violence.

For several years, MBA students in Duke's Fuqua School of Business were asked to write a personal strategic plan. The question posed to them was, "What do you want to be when you grow up?." With few exceptions, they wanted three things—money, power, and things—very big things, including vacation homes, expensive foreign automobiles, yachts, and even airplanes. Primarily concerned with their careers and the growth of their financial portfolios, their personal plans contained little room for family, intellectual development, spiritual growth, or social responsibility. Their mandate to the faculty was, "Teach me how to be a money-making machine." Their mandate to the faculty was not, "Show me how earning an MBA can lead to the meaning of life."

I fear that most of us are world-class conformists, who cannot get beyond ourselves to think seriously about what life means. Yet, the great thinker

Camus probed our mind when he said, "The meaning of life is the most urgent of questions." Rather than ask about this meaning of life, people are searching for the correct manila folder in which to get filed away.

Recently, a father inquired of his college-going son, "What are you trying to learn in your courses?" "I am trying to figure out the meaning of life," replied the son. With some astonishment and anger the father retorted, "That will not get you very far."

Little did the father know that asking ultimate questions might take his son farther than he would ever be able to go.

It is worth pondering.

# Clint's Hard Questions

Each and every Sunday, Clint sits on the same pew with my wife and two daughters. He's a real pistol. Clint is the six-year-old who is usually the first one to arrive for the children's sermon; usually the one who pops a question right in the middle of the sermon for children; usually the one who causes laughter to ripple through the congregation because of some inquiry or display.

Almost every Sunday afternoon Janene, Melanie, and Heather tell me something that Clint did or said during the worship hour. What they say he said is, more often than not, funny. Rarely sad. Never boring. And often insightful. There is one thing for certain, and that is that no one is certain what he will say next. Only the creative, free-floating mind of a child could shape the thoughts that pour like running water from Clint's lips.

My family is in love with Clint. In love with him because he is smart, cute, not a carbon copy of anyone you ever saw, and—most of all—because of his other uniqueness as a human being.

A few Sundays ago Clint came to our house for Sunday lunch. Before lunch he was all over the house and yard, exploring every nook and cranny. With every discovery he had a question or a comment. He was never quiet nor still, but was forever on the move and full of words. He darted around the house faster than Mark trotting from the choir loft to the back balcony.

When it came time to eat, we put Clint at the head of the table so that he could easily be seen and heard. Before eating a wonderful Sunday lunch, I offered to give thanks for the meal. I said, as I always do, "Make us thankful for this food and for all of our blessings. Amen."

In a split second after I had said "Amen," Clint called out, "Your sermons are too long and your blessings are too short. Why don't you have shorter sermons and longer blessings?"

Since my daughters time my sermons every Sunday, they got a big kick out of Clint's observations. "How are you going to answer that one, Dad?" asked one of my offspring. "I'm guilty," I responded. "My sermons are often longer than they need to be, and my prayers of thanksgiving are not large enough."

Clint is a child of the Church. He, unlike many children today, knows about worship, blessings, and sermons. By coming to church every Sunday, he is being formed in the faith. Concepts and beliefs are beginning to take shape in his life. His family, unlike many, has lived up to the vows that they took at his baptism. As he comes to church from Sunday to Sunday, he will learn something of his vocation as a Christian.

At every person's birth there comes into being an eternal vocation that is expressly for that person. To be true to oneself in relation to this eternal vocation is the highest thing that a person can practice. As the poet once said, "Self love is not so vile a sin as self neglecting."

Hopefully, the Church can teach Clint and all children that there is one great fault and offense: disloyalty to one's own self, or the denial of one's own better self. Hopefully, those of us who preach long sermons and have short blessings can help the Clints of this world to see themselves as God's children. When we see ourselves that way, better self begins to shine forth.

Thanks, Clint, for a wonderful Sunday afternoon, for being special, for asking hard questions, for being nice to my family, and for being who you are. Clint, as you grow older, you will discover the depth of faith that is in your lineage. My prayer is that you will discover your eternal vocation, which is, after all, the reason for your existence.

It's worth pondering.

# Love

# Kitchen Table Friends

Last Sunday evening some friends phoned to ask if they might come over for a few minutes. Said they did not want anything. Just wanted to check on how we were getting along. "Of course," I said, "we would be happy to see you."

After a short while the doorbell rang and in they came. Conversation started even before we could get seated before a pretty fire. Talk moved from topic to topic—our children, our respective congregations, a recently given birthday party, the George Bush family, and a cyst that I am to have removed from my head.

Before we knew it the time had come for supper. Janene offered a turkey sandwich. Our guests refused. She offered again. They said that they had not come to eat. I offered. Again they said, "No, we must go." Janene said, "It's just a turkey sandwich, and it will not take but a minute so please stay." They nodded "yes," and off we went to the kitchen for a great turkey sandwich and more conversation.

That's what we can do with our very best friends. We can serve them leftovers around the kitchen table.

Life does not offer us many kitchen table friends. And it is a sad and terrible thing when people cannot name one friend with whom leftovers can become a sacrament.

It's worth pondering.

# Obeying the Unenforceable

A few weeks ago I attended the Saturday morning session of the United Methodist Men's Retreat. Those who attended sought to interpret life from the vantage point of the Christian faith. I was intrigued as the roundtable discussion revolved around questions of ethics. Again and again we kept coming back to that foundational concern.

Ethics, like good music, is very difficult to define. But you know ethics when you see ethics. Ethical people have a certain resolve. They stand out. Without calling themselves "ethical," they live at a high level.

Lord Moulton Bank, a nineteenth-century parliamentarian, said that ethics is "obedience to the unenforceable." The test of a person is his or her obedience to that which one cannot be forced to obey. Ethical people are those who enforce unenforceable laws upon themselves.

They go further than those who do what they do because the lawmakers have ruled that they must. And ethical people take an ever higher road than those who adhere only to the domain of free choice. There is a higher ethic than living by laws written on books, and doing what one does because it expresses the freedom of the individual.

The "Christian ethic," as we call it, is rooted in two great traditions. One is Judaism. The other is the teaching of Jesus.

The great contribution of Judaism to the world was the concept of justice. Our Jewish heritage, as illustrated in the Hebrew Bible, has taught us to ask, "What is fair?" in every given situation.

If those two teachings are put side by side, we have the foundation for ethical living. In every situation we would do well to ask: "Is it fair?" and "Is it loving?" If an action is fair and loving, it is likely to be in accordance with the will of God.

The immorality of the 1980s—the greed, the hypocrisy, and the arrogance that has bubbled forth in both the public and private sectors—demands that we begin to raise serious questions about justice and love. There is no other way to maintain obedience to the unenforceable.

Why it is so difficult for us as a society and as individuals to obey the unenforceable is worth pondering.

# Simple, Yet Difficult

The Old Testament listed Ten Commandments. Jesus knew them by heart. No doubt He had rehearsed them in His mind more times than He could remember. He must have pondered their meaning and searched for an application of their intention for human life. They were riveted to His conscience.

Those who came to Him one day knew that He knew all ten of the commandments. But they wanted to know which of the ten He thought to be the most important. Hearing their question, Jesus said, "You shall love the Lord your God with all your heart, and with all your soul, and with all your mind. This is the greatest and first commandment. And a second is like it: You shall love your neighbor as yourself. On these two commandments hang all of the law and the prophets."

His answer has gone down in the annals of theology as the Great Commandment. It is simple. It is two-fold. It is easily memorized.

This commandment, "the Great One," is easy to learn and easy to understand, but it is very difficult to keep.

It is the way that life is supposed to be, but it is not so easy to make life work the way our Lord intended.

It is not easy to keep the Great Commandment, because we do not have within ourselves the power to do so. We do not have the strength, the will, nor the moral mettle to live up to this high standard. By our own muscle and wit we cannot live out the meaning of loving God and loving our neighbor.

But if we are going to love God and our neighbor, we must start someplace. We need to begin by admitting how difficult it is to love this way. Own it. Say it to ourselves. Say it to God.

The next step is very simple, but very difficult. We need to let God work through us. It is God working through us that enables us to love this way. If God does not move through us, it will be impossible to love God in the right way and to love our neighbor in the right way.

In a word, we need to be transformed by the Holy One if we are to keep this Great Commandment.

The very One who gives us the Greatest Commandment is the very One who enables us to keep it.

It is worth pondering.

# The Alternative

Violence wears many faces. It seems to stalk us at every turn. The evening news on television often begins with a lead story about some violent act. Newspapers are full with it. FBI statistics tell us that a violent crime was committed every twenty-two seconds in 1992.

The average American child will see 8,000 murders and 100,000 other acts of violence on television by the time he or she leaves elementary school, according to the figures reported by the American Psychological Association.

Examples of our struggle against violence are everywhere: built-in surveillance cameras; metal detectors; gadgets that screen out unwanted telephone calls; security guards at work places demanding to see employees' identification tags; brawls after sporting events in the name of fun or celebration; signs saying, "Driver carries only $5.00 in change"; car phones as bridges to safety; glass mirrors that you look into and wonder who is looking back.

In my judgment we focus too much on the act of violence and not enough on the cause of violence. Focus is, therefore, on the symptoms and not on the cure.

I have the fear that many who commit violent acts have never heard the demand for unconditional love made by Christ in the Sermon on the Mount, which calls for the renunciation of violence that destroys the existence, freedom, dignity, and happiness of others.

Had those who murdered the tourists in Florida ever heard about loving others?

Had those who slew the Nashville student over $20 at a Hillsboro Village bank ATM ever been taught that human life is sacred?

Do those who produce violent television episodes ever consider the devastating absence of love in such episodes?

Materialism, in whatever form, is not the answer to the raging violence. The answer is to be found in the realm of the spiritual, and it must take into account the notion that we are to "love our neighbors as ourselves."

Those of us who belong to the Church of Jesus Christ have taught this to each other and to our children, but we have not shared this great teaching with those beyond our faith circle, the TV producers, the boys who came to Hillsboro Village, or those who killed the tourists in Florida.

The alternative to violence is love. That is what we have to offer the world.

Why we have not done better at teaching what we have been taught is worth pondering.

# The Arrival of Love

I know a sixty-year-old man whose wife recently asked him for a divorce. She, according to her own testimony, had fallen in love with the next door neighbor, who happened to be a prominent person in the community. The divorce was very painful for both parties, but especially for the husband. For months he grieved over the loss of his wife to whom he had been married for about forty years. He complained of not feeling well. His place of business, an old filling station, got all run down and in need of basic repair work. His yard, once a showplace, started looking more like a weed patch. His car needed a good wash and a smooth coat of wax. He even complained of poor eyesight, but refused to go to the physician for much needed attention. He complained of a pulled muscle in his leg and, thereby, developed a noticeable limp.

About two years after the divorce this sixty-year-old person met a very attractive and thoughtful woman. Sparks flew. Feeling was there. They enjoyed the pleasure of each other's company.

Then a miracle happened. He decided to go to the eye doctor. He started taking regular exercise which eased the limp. His yard was cleaned and put back prettier than ever. The old service station got a new roof and a paint job. A new car was purchased. The grief passed, and he started living again.

Therein lies one of the oddities of human love. It has a unique and almost mysterious way of expanding and enlarging the human spirit. The freely given love of another person gives birth to something in us that cannot be contained. The barriers that we have erected to protect ourselves against disappointment and humiliation come tumbling down.

The one unmistakable sign of love that is true is the impulse it creates and the willingness to be renewed in our relationship to others.

Strange as it seems, the arrival of love in our lives gives us an entirely new image of ourselves. It helps us to believe that we must be wonderful, because someone wonderful loves us. Then, something else happens. Because we have a new image of ourselves, the rest of the world looks wonderful, too. Love has the power to change our perception of life and ourselves. It has the power to enlarge and expand us. When adequately loved, our love for life cannot be contained. It is not a burden. It overflows in a natural way.

A fundamental teaching of the Christian faith is that God loves us. In fact, God not only loves us, God delights in us, and yearns for us to accept divine love for ourselves, and to love others as God has loved us.

One day a lawyer asked Jesus, "What is the greatest commandment?"

Jesus responded by saying, "You shall love the Lord your God with all your heart, and with all your soul, and with all your mind. This is the great and first commandment. And a second is like it. You shall love your neighbor as yourself. On these two commandments depend all the law and the prophets."

How we are enlarged by such love is worth pondering.

# Solutions

E vents and happenings fill every day of our lives. A child has the first day of kindergarten. We ride in our car up and down the expressway. People call us on the telephone. Business deals are transacted. Letters are written. Computers are punched. A dog barks. Trees wave in the breeze. A job is lost. A child breaks faith. The grades are given. A relocation takes place. Events—one event after another—have a way of filling our lives.

A wise person once said that it is possible to have an experience and miss the meaning. So it is not the events that cross and criss-cross our lives that matter. Rather, it is the meaning that we bring to those events that ultimately matters.

We need more people in our society who will ask, "What do these events mean?" When the paper is read, the television is watched, and the news is heard, we need thoughtful people who will bring meaning to those events.

Take, for example, the horrible violence that we see displayed almost every day through the media and even with our own eyes. What does this mean and what does this tell us about the human condition? Does the violence tell us that we as the human family have now become depersonalized? Does it tell us that we see each other as "its" and not as "thous"? Or does it tell us that the sacredness of the human personality is not seen by many people in our culture? Or does it tell us that some people will use violence as a means to an end, which will bring either notoriety or prominence to themselves?

Certainly, violence tells us that there are multitudes in our culture who do not see other people as God sees them. Rather, the perpetrators of violence must see other people as a means to an end, as a way of getting what one wants, or as a way of bringing a cheap thrill into the dullness and humdrumness of some existence.

To put it bluntly, violence is telling us that life is not right. It is telling us that we have not yet learned how to love. It is telling us that a great void and vacuum exists in the lives of many people. It is telling us that many people in our society have not learned to live by the greater and more noble way of mercy, justice, and compassion.

What, then, is the answer to violence? I hold to the notion that the Christian faith has the answer to violence, and the answer to violence is sacrificial love, the kind of love that we see in the life and teachings of Jesus Christ. It is our task as the church to model a better and different way of life. A life that reflects the sacrificial love that is in Jesus Christ.

Almost everyone is looking for a solution to violence: politicians, educators, social scientists, psychologists, psychiatrists, family leaders. But in my judgment, we do not have to look for a solution to violence. That solution has already been given. It goes something like this. "Do unto others as you would have them do unto you."

It was spoken a long time ago by a man from Nazareth, even Jesus Christ. It's worth pondering.

# What We Live From

What we live from is very important. We cannot live from position or power, though many build their lives around both. Nor can we live from entertainment, though many of us are entertaining ourselves to death. Nor can we live from hard work, though many are slaves to our jobs. Nor can we live from art, though art has a way of opening meaning for us. Nor can we live from music, though music can bring heaven to earth. Nor can we live from family, though it gives joy and warmth. Nor can we live from literature, though it provides insight and pleasure. Nor can we live from sports, though sporting events provide interruption from the everydayness of life. Nor can we live from money, though for a fair number of people money has become god. Nor can we live from politics, though we need the proper ordering of life. All of these things have their place, but none of them is sufficient for life.

We can only live from love, because love is the only thing that cannot be destroyed. But it is not just any kind of love that makes life possible. It is sacrificial love that gives us something to live from.

In the life and teachings of Jesus we see an example of sacrificial love. When we sacrificially live for one another, we have something to live from. Practicing sacrificial love is not something that we can manufacture or produce. It comes from loving God, whose nature is love.

Why we have not laid hold of this important truth is worth pondering.

# What's Wrong with That?

His name was Montie; at least, that's what everyone called him. His head, feet, and hands were oversized when compared to the rest of his body. He always wore work clothes with a railroad hat perched on top of his head.

Montie was our volunteer "Mr. Fix-It" at the church that I was serving. He'd come over to the church almost every day to see what we needed to have painted or repaired. If a light switch would not work, we would say, "Let Montie fix it." No matter what—carpentry, plumbing, roofing, masonry, or painting—Montie would always tackle it.

So far as I know he never took a dime for his labor. All that he needed was a bunch of charge accounts at various supply houses, and he would get the job done. In addition, he was one of those rare people who cleaned up after himself.

If it was going to be a big job where he needed an extra pair of hands, he would bring Pearle with him. Pearle was his wife of some fifty years plus. Montie said that she was not a good worker, but that she was as good a helper as one would ever want.

There was one problem with Montie. It was not the quality of his work, nor the length of time it took, nor his attitude. The vexation with him was that no matter what he had accomplished, he would always want one of the clergy to look at what he had done. No matter what I was doing, Montie would interrupt me to "show off" what he had repaired. I could recognize his shuffling steps coming down the hall, and I knew that I was going to be pulled away from my labor to see the results of his labor. After showing me the job, his question was always the same: "What's wrong with that?" he would say, as he proudly pointed his long index finger at the job. The greater problem was that Montie would not wait until he had finished a task before he would drag me away from my desk to show me what he had done. He would paint one strip, fix one board, patch one hole, tighten one nut, repair one switch, and then he would take me, or whomever he could find, and ask, "What's wrong with that?" Ninety-nine percent of the time there was "nothing wrong with that," so all but one percent of the time was spent patting Montie on the back for a job well done.

Growth in God's Church occurs because there are many Monties—people who love the Church and who do what they can to enable it to continue the work of Christ on earth. "What's wrong with that?"

It's worth pondering.

# When Life Happens to Us

Most of us try with all that is in us to make life come out right. But despite all of our efforts, most of life happens to us. The big turning points do not happen because we sit in a long range planning committee, or because we anticipate the future. Most of the time the pivotal events in our lives come as the result of many interacting factors. We cannot forecast these factors, nor do we anticipate them. And more often than not, they are beyond our control.

Leander E. Keck, in his book *The Church Confident,* has reminded us that "no one planned the Protestant Reformation, the discovery of the two continents west of Europe and Africa, the slaughter that two worldwide wars turned out to be, or the collapse of the Soviet Union. The winds of history blow as they will, bringing the unexpected to pass and summoning us to adjust our sails as best we can. So too, no one planned the relentless and irreversible pluralization of the American populace."

Our Lord was no exception. To be sure, He made things happen in life. But life also happened to Him. The political and religious leaders turned against Him. The disciples deserted and denied Him. The billowing tide of history seemed to turn against His teachings and that for which He stood.

In the face of life turning against Him, Jesus kept the faith. He remained obedient to God. He did not blink.

When life turns against the grain, we, like our Lord, need to remain steadfast, true, obedient, and loyal to the God of Jesus Christ. Drawing upon and relying on our religious resources will get us through even the darkest hours of life.

At such times it is important for us to slow down, remember our values, trust friends, and believe with all of our heart that even the darkest hour is not the last hour.

The God who brought life from the cross is the same God who can bring hope and love to the crosses that we bear.

It's worth pondering.

# Prayer

# Another Kind of Health Care

L ast Wednesday evening the nation watched as President Clinton unveiled his health care plan. He spoke. The Republicans responded. Opinions started popping. Who knows where this process will lead us? In all of our discussions about this important question we, as Believers, would do well not to forget the spiritual resources that we have. I believe that spirituality is an important resource when we are trying to cope with physical, mental, or emotional illness. If we are spiritual beings who have a body, instead of bodies with spirits, then it is essential to understand the importance of acknowledging the spirit during a health crisis and the healing process.

As a pastor, I spend a portion of every week as a caregiver to those who are sick. Nonjudgmental, loving presence is an important part of that task. Active listening. Being empathetic. Caring. These are all essential if I am going to be supportive during these times.

It is also my custom to have prayer with those whose health has broken. Often I will pray something like, "Lord, we thank you for the miracles of modern medicine and for all of the persons and resources of this hospital. Be unto your servant as the Great Physician, and uphold her (or his) faith that she (or he) will not be afraid. May this your child trust you in sickness as well as in health. Continue, we ask you, to be part of the healing process until the health of mind, body, and spirit is restored. Forgive us of our sins, even as we put this illness in your hands. Amen."

Such prayer helps us to center our thoughts and emotions. It reminds us that there is also a spiritual dimension to the healing process. It affirms our belief that God participates in the healing process. And when I seriously pray for a sick person, I am put in touch with those who need, but do not have, adequate health care. Authentic prayer always leads us to human needs.

The spiritual side of health care is available to all. It does not require a speech by the president, nor does it need an act of Congress, or a new federal or state program. It is a grand resource that stands ready to be used.

Why some see the spiritual dimensions of health care and why some do not is worth pondering.

# Prayer for Sinners

The sign parked in the front yard of the small weather-beaten, rural church said, "Come Here Where Sinners Are Prayed For." I saw that lettering as I drove on a remote section of a Georgia highway while headed for Atlanta.

While staying at an Atlanta motel, I thumbed through the yellow pages looking for the address of a particular congregation. Located in the middle of one of those pages was an advertisement that invited people to an affluent church which offered a "Complete Recreational Program."

One church presented itself as being concerned about sinners, while the other congregation invited people to come for recreation.

In my opinion the plain one-room church had a clearer understanding of what it means to be the Body of Christ, than did the congregation that could afford to put a big advertisement in the yellow pages.

To be certain, there is a place for the recreation in the church, because all of us need to be "re-created" so that we might render greater service to God by being in service to others.

My concern is that in the modern church it can be easier to experience recreation than to find times and places where "sinners are prayed for." We sin each and every time that we fail to live in the fullness of Christ. Sin is any thought, word, or deed that caused us to fall short of what Christ achieved. This means that all of us are sinners, and that all of us, and all people everywhere, need to be "prayed for."

It is worth pondering.

# Prayer in Public Schools

I grew up in a white, Anglo-Saxon, Protestant community. In my public school there were no ethnics, because a rigid form of segregation was held firmly in place. To my knowledge there was one Jewish family in our school population. One of the Jewish sons was in my class from the first through the eleventh grade. His father owned a small dry goods store and the family lived upstairs.

For eleven years this Jewish boy listened to the morning homeroom devotional. Back in the '40s and '50s, it was a common practice for each homeroom to begin the day by having Bible reading and prayer. In our school the homeroom teacher would assign that responsibility to various students. Most of the time, as I remember, the students would read from the New Testament, and then lead the class in saying the Lord's Prayer.

I only remember one occasion when Jacob, my Jewish friend, was assigned the responsibility for offering leadership in the opening devotional exercises. He read the Torah, and invited the class to join him in saying the Shema. Both his reading and his invitation seemed strange to us. It did not fit our way of seeing life. It seemed out of place in a classroom that was accustomed to hearing words from the new covenant.

Somehow, conservative Christians in our school got all worked up because Jacob had imposed his religious beliefs on the rest of us. Said that Jacob had no right to use words and prayers that the rest of us did not understand. Said that this is a "Christian country," and that we needed to keep it that way. Said that Jacob needed to go to Central, which was where all the other Hebrews attended. Said that Treadwell was our school and that no foreign beliefs could be tolerated.

It is because of the Jacobs in our public life that I get uneasy when students are forced to be inculcated with particular religious beliefs (including atheism) in the public schools.

The basic tenets of religion and prayer should be taught by the church and the home. We, in my opinion, should not look to the public schools to teach a particular view of religion. At the same time, a student should be permitted to bow his or her head at any time during the day for voluntary prayer. Likewise, a student should be permitted to carry a New Testament, or a Torah, or a Book of Mormon for personal use at a time of his or her discretion. Likewise, the public schools should be very careful in requiring students to say a Jewish, Christian, or Islamic prayer. It should also be cautious in requiring students to repeat an atheistic or deist statement. Students should always feel free to voluntarily practice their cherished and particular religious convictions. But students should not be required to practice a particular religious persuasion.

Having said all of the above, I do believe that a well-worded and extremely sensitive prayer, which takes into account a great diversity of belief, is appropriate for highly significant occasions, such as commencement exercises. Such a prayer, in my view, is not inculcating on religion. It is the acknowledgement of the reality of the transcendent. If we pray in this way we are saying that there is a higher value than the principalities and powers of this world.

The end of such a purely secular position is not, "What is good?" or "What is just?" or "What is best for the larger community?" but, "Where's mine?"

It's worth pondering.

# Touchdown Prayers

Recently, our attention has been drawn to football players who kneel in the end zone after scoring a touchdown. According to some published reports, these prayers are merely thanking God for having the athletic ability to score points.

I am not one to question the motives or the theology of those who kneel after racking up points. But there is something about this "ritual" that causes me to reflect. Why is it that players do not drop on one knee after a player has been injured? Or, why do they not pray a prayer of thanksgiving for a substitute player who makes his first tackle in the first game in which he has ever played? Why do they not pray a prayer for forgiveness after an outpouring of profanity? Or why is there no prayer of sympathy and compassion for the disappointment of the losing team? Should public demonstrations of prayer only be for those times when points are scored?

One of the central teachings of the Christian faith is that we should pray for others first and ourselves last. Praying only after a winning touchdown reverses the natural order of prayer. It thanks God for an accomplishment, while forgetting to hold before God the hurts and hopes of others.

Praying after a touchdown says more about the Church's failure to teach the meaning of prayer than it does about athletes who are only being true to their understanding.

Let us pray that the Church will teach us how to pray.

# Unity, Not Sameness

Every Sunday morning I stand at the door of the Brentwood United Methodist Church sanctuary to greet those who are leaving worship. It is a good time for me, because words and feelings are exchanged. "Enjoyed the sermon." "Did you know that John Doe is in the hospital?" "Need to talk with you about a wedding." "Did you hear that my daughter got a scholarship?" "My wife has been diagnosed with cancer." "How did you like the game yesterday?" "Let's play golf." And on and on the questions go.

A few Sundays after I arrived as the senior pastor of this congregation, Mary said, "Pastor, I want you to know that I am praying for you. In fact, I pray for you every day." Aside from my mother, she is one of the few people who ever said that to me. It goes without saying that it felt good to hear those words, "I am praying for you." To know that someone is presenting my needs before God is both humbling and empowering. When we know that someone is praying for us, we do not feel alone. Instead, we feel solidarity with another person and that person feels "at ease" with us.

In one of His last prayers, Jesus did for us what Mary did for me. In His final prayer He prayed for those Believers who would come after Him. It is interesting to note that for which He prayed.

He did not pray that we (those of us who have followed after Jesus) would have prosperity, or peace of mind, or success, or opportunities. Of all things, He prayed that we would have unity. In a word, Jesus' final hope was that we, as His followers, would be unified with each other.

Here, He was not talking about the world, or nations, or cities, or communities. He was praying for those who would for generations name His name and take up His cross. But, more specifically, He was praying for today's Church. For you and me. For United Methodists. Baptists, Pentecostals, Roman Catholics. Unitarians. Snake handlers. He was praying that we would be unified with each other.

I believe that Jesus was praying for a spiritual unity and not a regimented union of churches. He was praying for the kind of unity that would encourage us to join hands and hearts in spite of our denominational differences.

He prayed that we would be one, even as He and the Father are one. This means that He wanted us to be tied to each other, even as He and God were bound to each other. He knew the power that came from that binding and He wanted us to have the same strength.

If Jesus prayed that we would be one, both His heart and the heart of God must be saddened by the divisions that exist in today's Church. Instead of working toward unity, there is in many quarters a polite *competitiveness* among the churches.

Last January I had the opportunity to join two of our neighboring pastors on a panel for Leadership Brentwood. We were each invited to talk about the outreach and program ministries of our respective congregations. Father Ed Alberts, of Holy Family Catholic Church, and the Reverend Mike Glenn, of Brentwood Baptist Church, and I each spoke about the contribution that our respective congregations are making to this community. The list of programs and ministries was very long and most impressive.

At the end of our presentation, the fire chief inquired about what we were doing together to make this a better community. Except for the community Thanksgiving Service, and minimal cooperation at the Counseling Center, we could not name specific ways that we are trying to impact this community with the life giving spirit of Jesus Christ. Since we know that to be true, we had to say it to Leadership Brentwood—though we had already said it with our actions.

Jesus did not pray that we would be separated. He prayed that we would be one even as He and the Father are one.

We are living in a time when our unity needs to be visible enough to challenge this community to believe in the Christ who can transcend our differences and make us one.

But there is a caution. As we become more and more one in the Spirit, we must not give up that which makes us distinctive. Every religious tradition has something that is distinctive to contribute to the many-colored quilt of God's creation.

In His prayers Jesus did not call us to sameness. He called us to oneness.

How to be one without being the same is worth pondering.

# Why Pray?

P rayer seems useless in a world that places so much value on being productive. We live in a society that builds its life around production. Since production has such a high priority, those who do not produce are not highly regarded. The nonproducers are often thought of as nonpeople: abandoned children, old people, the handicapped, the unemployed, street people, the poor. All of these are treated as if their life is of little consequence. We value people by what they can make of their job, which, in turn, contributes to society. Therefore, prayer seems to be a time away from the real business of life. In the eyes of many people, prayer does not produce that which is tangible, so it must be of little value.

In my opinion, prayer is not about production. It is about having a shared life with God. It is a way of being present with God.

We are created to have a relationship with God. Prayer is the way that our relationship with God is kept alive. More than kept alive, it is the way that such a union grows and is strengthened.

Looking at a human analogy might help. If earthly families are to have deepening relationships, there must be times when family members are present with each other. If there is constant, persistent absence, relationships tend to break down. If families do not share their lives with each other, there is no growth in the family bond.

One of the reasons to pray is to strengthen and keep strong our shared life with God. There may be other good reasons, but this is the most important. It is worth pondering.

# Preaching

# Just the Biscuits

Aside from pancakes, popcorn, scrambled eggs, and something on the grill, I have never cooked anything worth writing home about. However, two weeks ago my luck changed. Janene's Sunday School class, the Joyful Noise Class, had a Valentine's dinner where the husbands were required to prepare and bring a dish. Since I could not take pancakes, popcorn, or scrambled eggs, I was in a bind. I told Janene that I would fix babyback ribs on the grill as my offering to the class. However, after studied and due consideration, I decided that the clock would not allow the necessary preparation time for such a refined southern delicacy.

Realizing my plight, Janene dug in her recipe box, pulled out an index card, and said, "Maybe you can make this. It is easy." The recipe that she handed me was for a dessert called "Preacher's Coming." It is one of those desserts that has an over-abundance of chocolate, nuts, wafer crumbs, egg yolks, sugar, and vanilla ice cream.

At first I was a bit confused. Her recipe called for "conf. sugar" so I asked if we had any "confederate sugar." It called for crushed vanilla wafers, so I used my fingers instead of the blender. It called for rolling them in the egg whites, so I tried to roll them in a glass before beating them into the bowl. It called for butter, so I used margarine. It called for a sprinkling of pecans, so I "sprinkled" them until they formed a solid top layer like a non-seethrough roof.

After working for four times as long as it was supposed to take, I finished my project and put it in the freezer until party time. When the evening finally arrived, all of the dishes were spread on the table for judging. The women went from dish to dish, tasting and talking in order to try to determine which recipe would take home the prize. After sampling all of the fare, a vote was taken to identify the winner.

You could have knocked me over with a broom straw when I was awarded a set of measuring spoons for having made the winning dessert. I won, though I could not read the recipe, could not get the measurements straight, and could not properly identify the ingredients.

Just goes to show you that we often win in spite of the mistakes that we make. It was the taste, not the recipe that ultimately mattered.

The Reverend Kelly Miller Smith, pastor of First Baptist Capitol Hill, was a good friend of mine. When we would see each other at Vanderbilt Divinity

School, or over lunch, we would often talk about the art of sermon preparation. Dr. Smith was fond of saying, "Joe, when you preach, always give your congregation the biscuits and never the recipe. They do not care about what's in the recipe. All they want is something to chew on."

Those of us who name the name of Christ have something to give the world, not always because of, but in spite of the ingredients that have gone into our lives.

How and when we give what we have to give is worth pondering.

# The Relentless Return

I have been giving sermons for over thirty years. In spite of the longevity, there is something that I understand and do not understand about the Sunday sermon. I understand that the effects of a sermon cannot be programmed. I do not understand how God uses the sermon for holy purposes. The results are more like a mystery than a fact.

Some Sundays I leave the pulpit feeling that the message of the Word has been truly communicated and received. People got it. Believers were held. The congregation was moved. I could see it in their eyes. Often, I would later discover that I had not been very effective.

But on other occasions I tried my best, but got mixed up on what I wanted to say—it just would not come together—and I stumbled over my words, and I knew that minds were wandering because people looked away, or because their eyes were glazed over. Those were the times when the sermons had the greatest impact. Those bungling sermons, I sometimes found out afterward, helped someone to do what he or she had been trying to do for a long time—reconcile with a friend, break with a bad habit, make a long delayed commitment, be more open to God, get to a counselor, or speak out against injustice.

Preaching has taught me that God continues to use the weak things of this world for His own purpose; and sometimes the weaker I feel, the more powerful God is. In preaching, Jesus continues to ride into Jerusalem on the back of a donkey.

I have a feeling that when people listen to a sermon they look at the preacher and ask, "Does this person really believe?" And, if the preacher believes, what effect does this have on his or her life? Is the preacher a stronger, more honest, more loving person as a result? It seems that we feed off of the faith of each other.

The members of the congregation seem to strengthen their own faith by nourishing themselves on the faith of the preacher. But the reverse is also true. The response of the people to the Word that he or she preaches does great things for the faith of the one doing the preaching.

I must quit writing *PONDERINGS* because Sunday is coming and yet another sermon must be given. I understand how to write the sermon. I do not understand how or if God will use it.

It is worth pondering.

# What Shall We Do with the Teacher?

Two Sundays ago I was shaking hands with people following the 10:55 AM worship service. Hand after hand. Person after person. Greeting after greeting. Name after name. Visitors. Members. Introductions.

Right in the midst of it all, I shook the hand of Leander Keck; a man who had, and continues to have, a profound influence on my life. When I was a student at Vanderbilt Divinity School 1961–64, he was my professor of New Testament.

I still remember his classes. Students filled almost every chair. I do not remember a class of his "not making." His lectures were always thoughtfully prepared and delivered with passion. He was eager for us to learn what he had discovered to be true. In his classes the message and the meaning of the New Testament came alive for me. Until this day I find myself asking, "What would Keck say about this?"

I can still recall the last day of the last class that I took under him. Students filled every seat, and some had to stand along the walls and sit on the window ledge. Anticipation filled every corner of the room. I do not remember the content of his final lecture, but I do remember how we responded. After his final sentence, there was a long silence, and then the class broke out in a sustained applause. The clapping was not boisterous. It was loaded with appreciation, almost reverent.

Keck acknowledged our response by nodding, picking up his lecture notes, Bible, and walking with head slightly bowed toward the door. Those of us who had L. E. Keck knew that we had been taught by a great teacher, whose influence would continue to instruct us for years to come.

At the time, I felt that Keck would move forward to distinguish himself in the field of New Testament studies. Since those early 1960s there has been lecture after lecture, book after book, article after article, and responsible position after responsible position. Most recently, he has been the dean of the Yale Divinity School.

It was this man, L. E. Keck, who sat in the congregation two Sundays ago. As I drove home from worship, I wondered what he thought about the sermon, the worship experience, the congregation, and, most of all, my interpretation of the New Testament lesson. Like all great teachers, he has helped to set within me a very high standard; one that was and was not met on the Sunday after Easter.

All able teachers continue to call us to our best effort. Their influence will not let us go. If we have two or three such teachers over the period of a lifetime, we have been given a precious gift.

In his own passionate way, Dr. Keck pointed us to *The Teacher* from Nazareth. In so-doing, the teacher from Vanderbilt Divinity School invited us to either affirm or reject the message of *The Teacher*.

# Sin

# A World of Our Own

Who can read the newspaper and watch the evening news without believing in sin? The world is not getting better and better as some would have us to believe. Nor is society moving from good to better to best.

All of us, says Christian theology, are so mired in sin that we cannot escape its power without the help of God. Sin is the religious corruption of one's existence. It is whatever act, attitude, or course of life that betrays God's intent for a human being. It is any thought, word, or deed that separates us from God or from one another. Sin is real and it is powerful and it cannot be explained away.

Our bent toward sin tells us something about the way that God has chosen to work. God has elected to work in such a way that we can interfere very drastically with His creation. God has made us such that we can rebel and set up our own "world" in opposition to God's highest purpose for us.

On the other hand, God knows that we can never be satisfied with any world of our own desiring, so that we will always be vulnerable to God's influence in one way or another—and God uses this "lack" to the full. But God always respects the freedom and independence given to us by God.

It is worth pondering.

# Sin Is . . .

I cannot adequately speak about sin without first speaking about what it means to live under the dominion of God. People of faith understand that we are intended to be subdued and dominated by divine love. If faith is to be consciously lived as if love rules our life, then sin means that something other than God has dominion over our life. It means that something other than God's loving will is allowed to have sway over us.

When we do not allow the divine to rule, we are selfishly directed toward ourselves. Such self direction leads to egocentricity, which is opposite to the divine will and, therefore, sin. Whenever egocentricity rules, our fellowship with God is destroyed. Whenever egocentricity rules, divine love does not and cannot rule, which is one way to look at the nature of sin.

In I Corinthians 13:5, St. Paul tells us that the characteristic of divine love is that it "seeketh not its own," which is the exact opposite of sin. The essence of sin is seen when our life is focused on "seeking our own way."

This seeking of our own way appears in many forms. It can even appear in our seeking after God, if such seeking attempts to secure something for one's own benefit by divine help. When we use God to fill our egocentric needs, sin is present in its most sublimated and deceptive form. Sin is, therefore, practiced when we do not live under the dominion of God's love, and when we try to make God the servant of our human desires and purposes.

If sin is "seeking our own way," instead of living under the dominion of God, St. Paul was right on target when he said that "all have sinned and fallen short of the glory of God." We are so mired in sin that we cannot extricate ourselves from its hold on us. Only God can deliver us and free us, and that is where we need to place our trust. Thus, it is faith in the grace of God that redeems us. Human effort will not do it. It is only human trust in God's love that will redeem and set free.

It is worth pondering.

# Spiritual Arrogance

At times I suffer from spiritual and theological arrogance. Hidden beneath the shadow of my soul is the misguided feeling that I know more than others about prayer, meditation, theology, the Bible, and the nature and purpose of the Church. It bothers me that I give myself permission to feel this vain superiority. As disturbed as I become about this feeling, I am far more disturbed about the enormous abyss between my insights and my life. In short, I know more than I am able to live out. Living by what we know to be true is not always easy.

To be even more candid, there are times when I feel imprisoned by my own insights and "spiritual competence." Feeling that I have gone beyond others in spirituality does not join me to others nor to God—it separates me.

If I do not want to be separated from God or from God's people, I need to learn and practice the openness that comes with humility. To learn to say "Lord, have mercy on me, a sinner" is more important than feeling my spiritual oats.

Though I feel this gap between what I know about God and what I am able to practice, I do want to grow in my love for God and all of God's people. One of the ways to close the gap is by seeing myself as a steward of all of the gifts that I have been given. To understand stewardship is to know that every action, even the smallest one, is part of the total action of God in life.

Wanting to grow into the fullness of the Christian life is not the same as believing oneself to be spiritually stronger than others.

How to tell the difference is worth pondering.

# The Danger of Green Grass

"And they lived happily ever after" is not in the Bible. In the Bible, people did not live happily ever after. That's Hollywood stuff, not biblical material. The children of Israel believed that they would live happily ever after if they could just get to the Land of Promise.

But, when the Israelites got to the Promised Land, they were greeted with new problems. They had to live among a foreign people called "Canaanites." These Canaanites had a different tongue, different customs, and different gods.

As soon as the Israelites crossed the Jordan, they discovered new problems that had to be solved. In a word, there was not much promise in the Promised Land.

When I was an associate pastor, I would often think about what I would do if I became a senior pastor. Toward the end of my tenure as an associate I had my opportunity. Dr. James A. Fischer, my senior pastor, had to be away for three weeks, and I was given full responsibility for the congregation. Within two hours of his departure everything looked different. It was one thing being on the sidelines looking in—it was quite another matter to "be in charge," as they say. I quickly discovered more and bigger problems than I had anticipated.

That is what happened to the Israelites; the grass was not as green as they had anticipated.

It is that way with the victor in a political election. On the night of the election, joy reigns. The next morning the newly elected official is brought face-to-face with the real problems that need to be solved. Suddenly, things are not as black-and-white and as cut-and-dried as had been previously thought.

When Joshua led the children of Israel into the Promised Land, the Israelites had three choices in dealing with their new problems. They could worship the past and go back to Egypt; they could worship and serve the gods of the Ammonites; or they could serve Yahweh, the God of Israel. And, likewise, the choices are ours.

We can worship the past. Immigrants to America have often come to the USA, only to make great efforts to re-create the past with Chinatowns, Little Italys, or Jewish ghettos. These people have moved physically, but not emotionally.

Likewise, when faced with new problems, congregations can worship the past. "Remember what it was like when so-in-so was pastor?" "Remember when we all believed the same things and shared the same vision?" "Remember when not as many people wanted to come to 'our' church?" Lessons from the past can inform and guide us, but we cannot worship the gods of the past any more than the Israelites could return to Egypt.

Our second choice is to worship the way other people worship. In so-doing, we give permission for the lords of the present to shape our lives. In my view, winning is almost a religion in America. There is no virtue in being Number 2. If you cannot say that you are Number 1, you are considered a failure. Many people feel they if they are not part of the largest, fastest growing, or biggest, they have probably missed catching the golden ring. If we worship the way other people worship, becoming successful will become our god! All of us should strive to do our best, but that might not put us at the top of the heap.

Our final choice is to live for God's future. God's future is not a future that we acquire, it is a future that we receive. No one can predict the future. It is beyond our forecasting abilities. The future will take us down many roads and around many unpredictable turns, but it is God's future to give and not ours to invent. Those who say with Joshua, "As for me and my house, we will serve the Lord," know that a primary loyalty to God will diminish the need to serve the gods of the past or the present.

It's worth pondering.

# The Herod Within

It took six trials before Jesus got his final sentence of death by crucifixion. Herod was one of those who took part in the ploy to put Jesus to death. Herod was cruel, cunning, lustful, and gullible. He believed in mesmerism, sports, and tricks. He practiced cruel incest. A sense of power possessed him. Half drunk, he had John beheaded.

When Herod put searching questions to Jesus, our Lord "answered him nothing." Why did the Nazarene not answer? Was it the silence of resignation? Or ignorance? Or fear? Or did Jesus not have an answer that would satisfy the likes of Herod?

Did ever two such extremes meet as when Jesus stood before Herod? On the one side there is the lowest imaginable form of human immorality. On the other there is Jesus—God's parable for how life ought to be. Pure servanthood standing before corrupt authority. That is the scene that will never be blotted from the grit and stars of eternal history.

So, why did Jesus have his lips locked into a blank silence? Could it be that he did not answer because he saw that Herod was so evil and so wrapped up in himself that he could not "hear"?

Perhaps Herod symbolizes all those who are so curved in upon themselves that they could not hear Christ if the Holy One decided to speak.

It is worth pondering.

# Worth and Winning

We are not the creators of the order in which we live. There is One who has made us, and not we ourselves. Built into the order of things is a pattern of righteousness that cannot be ignored. If we persist in breaking the laws of the universe, we will break against them. If we go against God's intended pattern, we will get splinters.

With this in mind, let us never forget that the Game of Life and its rules are more important than winning or losing.

A generation ago Grantland Rice said, "It is not whether you win or lose; it is how you play the game." However, the philosophy of Grantland Rice has now been supplanted by another dictum, Vince Lombardi's words, "Winning is not everything, it is the only thing."

Many of our problems today grow out of the Lombardi "theology," which has now become a national philosophy. Winning has become an obsession with us. When this happens, it is not surprising that the rules get bent, while any means are used to secure the goal. This disease is spreading through our whole society.

A few years ago the World Football League distorted their attendance figures in order to seem more successful than they were. Congregations often get obsessed with attendance figures, not because individual souls are cared about, but because there is a need to prove success by posting winning numbers. Individuals will magnify income as a way of proving to be winners. Companies will show a false bottom line because the need to be in the winners circle is so great.

Let us not forget that playing the Game of Life is really what matters, not just winning at any price. The Christian gospel tells us that our final worth as persons is not determined by how we come out in this or that competitive race.

Our worth is determined by the content of our character, our service to others, and our desire to love God and neighbor.

We should rightly admire those who achieve and accomplish, but we should never let the "wins" of others draw us into winning at any price.

Winning at any price causes us to falsely believe that there are "little sins" and "big sins." But, there are no little sins and big sins, only sin and virtue. Losing sight of this fact can get us into a big mess.

It is worth pondering.

# Special Days

# Teachers and Christ the King!

Today a great deal is being said and written about the importance of a better educational system for our children. In the state of Tennessee we have had the "Better Schools Program" the "Career Ladder Emphasis," and now Governor McWherter is wanting his final four years in office to be "For the Children."

Though I applaud all of these efforts, I feel ill at ease with the implication that our schools are filled with teachers who are not well trained and half-committed to their task.

I know an elementary teacher who taught all day every day last week, took care of her family, attended to responsibilities with her husband, came to church on Wednesday evening and Sunday morning, and worked until 9:30 each evening grading papers and doing lesson plans. She also attended an open house at her school for prospective students from 3:00 to 5:00 PM on Sunday afternoon.

The list of responsibilities continues. On Friday evening she attended a school party for her fifth and sixth grade students. Refreshments were served, games were played, and something that I still do not recognize or understand called "dancing" was enjoyed by all.

Though she is now fifty years of age, she participated in the "balloon pop" with her students. That's the game where balloons are tied around the ankles and the players attempt to stomp out the balloons of others, while not getting theirs mashed out. To say that it is a lively and energetic activity would be a gross understatement. But, there she was—right out there in the middle of the multitude—jumping and stomping and popping for all she was worth.

She spotted a boy in the throng who had done well on a test that had been taken earlier that day. She knew that he was anxious about the outcome, so she sought out the lad and whispered, "You made an 'A' today." He smiled with joy, not knowing that his teacher found the greater satisfaction in his accomplishment.

One of her students yanked a one dollar bill out of his pocket and said, "Could I buy you a Coke? I want to buy you a drink. Come on, come on, let's go now! I'll pay for it." His love and appreciation for her filled every word and expression. Such love for his teacher did not come because his teacher just did the minimum as a matter of routine. He was drawn to her because of something more than "reading, writing, and arithmetic." It was the relationship that caused him to say, "Could I buy you a Coke?"

As the evening wore on, the teacher listened to her students, entered into their world, spoke their language, and gave attention to their needs.

But it was not all fun. Panic struck her heart when it was discovered that one child had left the school grounds. Teachers and security guards got involved in the search. Roads were chased. Rooms were searched. Grounds were covered. Great was the relief when he was found. Still greater was the pain in knowing how to deal creatively with the situation.

At 10:00 PM the last student was picked up by a parent. As the teacher crawled into the car, her husband knew that it had been a long time since she had rolled out of bed at 6:00 AM.

And all that had happened between 6:00 AM and 10:00 PM is enough to fry the best of brains and to try the strongest of souls.

Let's be very careful when we talk about teachers. The ones that I know are hard working, committed to children, steadfast in their vision, and eager to go far more than the extra mile.

I see the labor poured into long days and nights. I see the agony when a child does not do well on a test. I see the extended preparation for parent conferences. I see the excitement when a child catches on and begins to move forward.

I know this because my wife, Janene, is a teacher. She gets her back up every now and then, and for twenty-eight years she has been trying without success to polish me up. She can be rather "forthright" when someone takes advantage of her or someone she loves, and when she gets her "dander up," you had better watch out! But she is a good teacher who loves her students and is loved by them.

Sunday is "Christ the King Sunday." It is a time when the Church affirms the Lordship of Christ in the world and in the lives of individuals. As the last Sunday in the Christian year, it is the prelude to Advent.

What motivates Janene and countless others in her profession is that they see students as a precious gift—a gift to be received, loved, and nurtured even as God has loved us.

How such relates to "Christ the King" is worth pondering.

# To Forgive or Bless

"Reflection" is a big and important word for the New Year. To use this time to reflect on that which is important and that which is not so important could be very helpful as we move into 1993. In last Monday morning's devotional reading, I came across a sentence from *The Christian's Secret of a Happy Life* by Hannah Whitall Smith. It said, "Never indulge, at the close of an action, in any self-reflective acts of any kind, whether of self-congratulation or of self-despair. Forget the things that are behind the moment they are past, leaving them with God."

I, for one, need to hear and heed that insight because I have trouble forgetting any performance or service rendered. My tendency is to indulge myself in evaluating, rehearsing, and replaying some moment that has already gone by. Rather than relive the words or deeds, I would do better if I honestly turned them over to the Lord to overrule my mistakes and to bless my efforts as He chooses. If I could do this simple thing, there would be fewer "blue Mondays" or times of depression.

For example, I have spent a fair portion of almost every Monday reworking the Sunday sermon. I think about questions like, "Was I true to the text?" "Could I have found a better illustration or quote?" "What could have gone unsaid?" "Was the good news proclaimed?" After considering questions like these, I often feel that I could preach a better sermon on Monday than on the preceding Sunday.

This is not to say that we should not evaluate our past actions and decisions. But it is to say that we should not make every effort to keep our past as current as the morning paper.

Why we will not render our past life unto God for the Holy One to either forgive or bless is worth pondering.

# Another "Million Man" March

This one is for men. White men. Black men. Men of every tribe, nationality, and skin pigmentation. I detest and reject Farrakhan's brand of racist, sexist, and antiSemitic bigotry. But I do respect those men who marched in Washington out of concern for their own families, their own children, and their own communities.

In my judgment our society needs another march by the men of this nation. The need is for men who will

- March off golf courses and tennis courts on Sunday mornings to worship God with their families
- March away from the work place a bit earlier so they can have an evening with those they love
- March away from a vacuum inside that persistently sucks up an infinite supply of thrills, goods, and success without satisfying the deepest longing of the human heart
- March toward God by participating in a small group that is intended for spiritual formation and for holding one another accountable
- March toward mentors who can help men to keep clear about what is important and what is trivia
- March toward integrity in personal and social relationships
- March away from words and actions that do not contribute to racial harmony
- March toward filling the hunger for greater spiritual depth and vitality
- March toward reflecting on life from the vantage point of the Christian faith
- March toward being physically and emotionally present with their children
- March toward setting an example by being good stewards of time, talents, and treasures

This march is more demanding and difficult than going to Washington for a day. It is an every hour of every day march. If we are to march with vigor and determination, we will need to practice the presence of God, and we will need to be present with each other.

It is worth pondering.

# Not Because We Are Good

Sunday we will be observing All Saints Day. It's a time for us to call to remembrance those who have died since last All Saints Day. But it is also a time for us to reflect on and call to mind those famous and not so famous men and women, and boys and girls, who have borne the light of Christ in their lives. It's now time to recall those persons who have been there for us in good times and bad—persons who have helped to see the light of Christ displayed.

My list of saints includes my wife and children, my parents and my extended family, a farmer from Chester County, a half-Indian history professor at Lambeth College, and more than one parishioner who wanted little else but to continue the work of Christ on earth. These are they who have been "Christ" for me. Together, we have shared the hurts and hopes of life. In a mysterious way the spirit of Christ has transcended our difference and made us one.

This Sunday we will call the roll of those who have been transferred to the Church Eternal since last year. We will read each name with an unmatched feeling of praise and thanksgiving—not because they were perfect, but because the light of Christ has shone through their lives.

And as we recall each name, we will remember that we are redeemed, not because we are good, but because God is loving.

It's worth pondering.

# The Importance of Saturday and Sunday

They sat two tables away from me. And they sat side by side. They ate their sausage and biscuit as if they were inhaling, not chewing. Both were dressed in baseball uniforms, complete with matching caps and shirts. They were obviously eager about the game that was to be played that morning. As I watched them and listened to them talk baseball, I puzzled about what was going on between that father and son.

Appearances would say that they had a lot in common. Baseball. Saturday morning breakfast. The sheer pleasure of sharing some time together. The father seemed to know what his son was thinking and feeling, and the son seemed pleased that his dad had crawled over into his "little league" world.

As I watched them prepare for the day, I puzzled about what their relationship might become. Would they always hold something in common or would they drift apart? Would they grow in their relationship with the passing of time or would it diminish? Would they always enjoy Saturday morning breakfast, baseball and just spending some time together? Would there be something or someone that brought mutual satisfaction to both?

Or would something or someone come between them? Would the son become shaped by a different story? A story not known or understood by his father? A story filled with different characters shaped around a vague and obscure plot? A story whose ideology ran contrary to the values and beliefs of the father?

Would the father's life become shaped by a different story? A story that involved another woman? Another job? Moving to another part of the country? A story that contained fewer convictions and a lessened understanding of what life really means? A story that had less talk and more action or more action and less talk?

Would the son grow up and live his life apart from the influence of his father? Or would he grow up and develop a dependent relationship? Would the relationship remain strong and vital in spite of the competing stories that would shape the life of each?

There is also the possibility that the smaller stories of the father and son would someday be connected to a larger story that would give meaning and purpose to life. If both become shaped by a larger story, it does not really matter how the script to the smaller story is written.

The next day, I saw the same father and son sitting side by side in the sanctuary. They sang together, read together, listened together, took the bread and the cup together, and together they held hands as the congregation sang, "Blest Be The Tie That Binds." In so-doing they were being shaped by the story that gives ultimate meaning to all of the tiny stories.

The father has his priorities right. He knows that it is important to be with his son while playing ball on Saturday, and to share worship with his son on Sunday. Neither one to the exclusion of the other.

I know of other fathers who join their sons in holding the bat and glove, but rarely, if ever, join their sons in holding the hymnal, the bread, and the wine.

Why so many fathers do one without the other is worth pondering.

# Our Burden and Blessing from God

For slightly over thirty years I have been standing behind oaken pulpits in United Methodist churches. And rarely in that span of time have I attempted to preach a typical Mother's Day sermon. There are many reasons for my attempt to avoid sermonizing about mothers.

In the first place, I have been more concerned about the calendar of the church year, than about having the secular calendar imposed upon the lectionary of the church. In a word, I have not wanted Hallmark, the advertising companies, and the floral industry to set the agenda for the sermon. Rather, I want the Sunday sermon to grow out of the Biblical word, as opposed to the cultural season.

But there have been other reasons that I have taken this trail. I am aware that many who listen have been hurt by their mothers so that the typical Mother's Day homily does not fit. Likewise, there are many single persons who yearn to be married so that they can have a family, and I have wanted to be sensitive to their needs. I have also been alert to those in the congregation who feel estranged and alienated from this one who is a significant other.

Over these years I have also learned that there are a few mothers in every Mother's Day congregation who are not remembered. A telephone call does not come. Flowers do not arrive. A note is not written. Often, that forgotten mother will come to worship and sit behind a mother who is bedecked with a corsage and a new dress, and who is sitting in the midst of a pew full of children.

Or perhaps I have merely reacted against the Mother's Days of my childhood. One of my childhood pastors had the habit of recognizing certain mothers on Mother's Day. He would give a flower to the oldest mother, the youngest mother, the newest mother, the mother who had given birth to the most children, and the mother who had the most grandchildren. My pastor's emphasis was always on procreation, and not on the content and quality of one's life as lived before God and others.

But for reasons known only to the heart, my mind has changed. This year I am going to preach a sermon that I hope will be fit for Mother's Day. In revaluing the Mother's Days that have come and gone, I have decided that I have possibly thrown out the baby with the bath water.

Given the current situation, a word needs to be said for, about, and to mothers. I hope that it will be a word of both truth and grace.

In revaluing motherhood I want us to look at the qualities that were found in Mary, the mother of Jesus. For United Methodists, Mary is not to be worshipped as a god, but she is to be admired, yea, even imitated as a mother. What she did in response to God was a heroic act of courage and trust. We would do well to look at what came of her faithfulness. It was not a life of ease for her, to be sure—that is never the shape that the favor of God assumes.

Jesus must have learned something from Mary. He must have learned to live with the burden and blessing that comes with being favored of God.

What we can learn from Mary about motherhood and about faithfulness is worth pondering.

# The Most Free Are the Most Bound

L ast week we passed through the Fourth of July in the accustomed way. Parades. Fireworks. Picnics. Family. A day off. Barbecue. Camping. Reading. A short trip. But, as a wise person once said, "We had the experience and missed the meaning." And it is a meaning that is not confined to the Fourth of July, as symbolic and important as that is.

Freedom is a big word for this season. Reflecting on the "freedoms" of our country has driven me to a deeper consideration of freedom. Allow me a few observations.

First, empty freedom is a snare and a delusion. If I follow only what comes naturally and easily, life simply ends in confusion and in possible disaster. Being free from responsibility does not lead to fulfillment. Being free from that which we do not prefer does not always lead to accomplishment.

Sometimes I allow myself to believe that life would be better if I could give all of my thought and effort to only that which catches my fancy. If I would only chase my interests. If I could figure some way to avoid the diversions and the interruptions. If I could get rid of the roadblocks. As much as I would like to be free from all that I do not like, I know that life is not that way. St. Paul reminds us that we all have our thorn in the flesh. There is something objectionable, difficult, and not preferable to all of our life and work.

For example, I do not like committee meetings. Some people relish them. Not me. In fact, I have often said that "If there are committee meetings in heaven, I do not want to go." I would rather be reading, writing, shepherding, helping, visiting, preaching, parenting, selfing, golfing, gardening, husbanding, vacationing—almost anything more than another meeting.

But after thirty years in the pastorate, and enough meetings to clog a good computer, I have discovered (much to my amazement), that God can even work through a meeting to accomplish some divine purpose. The very thing that we would like to be free from might be the one issue that needs our attention. So we dare not be soft and indulgent with ourselves. Excellence comes at a price, and one of the major prices is to learn to use our freedom to handle wisely and well those necessary evils that are part and parcel of life.

Secondly, there is a paradox to freedom. That paradox is that the most free are the most bound. But not just any way of being bound will suffice; what matters is the character of our binding. For example, the one who would like to be a good organist, but who is unwilling to discipline the body by regular practice and by foregoing some things, will not be free to excel at the great keyboard. And so with an athlete. If one does not train rigorously, one is denied the freedom to go over the bar at the desired height, or to run the desired speed and endurance.

That which is true for the athlete and the organist is also on target for the spiritual life. I must say, as senior pastor of Brentwood United Methodist Church, that too many of our Believers want a vital spirituality without the disciplines of worship, Scripture reading, receiving the sacraments, prayer, and bearing one another's burdens. For too many, Church has become optional. For too many, discipline has been replaced by convenience. John Wesley, the founder of Methodism, said that all Believers should "avail themselves of the means of Grace." He meant that we should avail ourselves with discipline and devotion, which alone gives freedom to live out the Gospel.

When it comes to a strong life and a vital religion, discipline is the price of freedom!

It's worth pondering.

# Spiritual Growth

# A Mature Faith

The words "spirituality" and "spiritual growth" are on the lips of many people today. And rightly so, because our concern for the world and for others needs to grow out of a deeply rooted piety. If we are to grow spiritually, we must not lose sight of some simple requirements.

The first is that life is a gift and not an entitlement. To see life as a gift is to stand in "awe" of life. It is to receive life, to succor life, and to rejoice in life.

The first and most important gift is God's gift of himself in Jesus Christ. The second most important gift is the gift of ourselves and the unique gifts that belong to each of us. These gifts are given, not that we might use them for our own benefit, but for the benefit of others.

The second requirement is that of love. Not any kind of love, but an openness and a readiness to accept God and other people into one's heart. Christianity has often been called the school of love. Those who grow spiritually are those who have a deep commitment to the art of loving. So we, as Christians, are lovers who hold our friends in the love of God.

The third requirement is discernment. Discernment is to thoroughly know oneself. It is to be aware of my own sinfulness and silliness, and at the same time to be aware of the amazing and forgiving love of God, which is available to me at all times. To discern is to be penitential and joyful at the same time: penitential because we discern how far we have all fallen short of the glory of God; joyful because the glory still outshines our failure to honor it. Discernment is the gift of hearts that try to read life and its relationship to God.

The fourth requirement is that of patience. Patience takes courage. It takes the courage to be still and wait. This is a difficult thing to do in our activist culture. For us, "doing" is more important than "being." Being busy before the Lord is more important than waiting for God.

Finally, if we are to grow in the spiritual life, we must be willing to embrace solitude and cultivate detachment, so that we might become more available to what God and the Holy Spirit are doing in the human heart. Not many of us are driven by what we experience in solitude and detachment. We are driven by the blaring banal voices and clanging sounds of this generation.

Mature faith does not come quickly like instant potatoes. It comes to us on the long, winding path of love, discernment, patience, and solitude. But, it begins by truly believing that life is a gift.

It's worth pondering.

# A Spiritual Journey

L ately, I have been on a spiritual journey. It is not a fad or another "kick" in yet a different direction. Something profound is stirring inside of me. I would like to tell you about it. It started about two months ago. I came to a time when I wanted to know more about Joe Pennel. I had a desire to go inside myself to see if I could discover the person within the person. I wanted to meet the person who is uniquely me. I had a need to find my own voice.

My journey has taken me up and down the relational roads of my childhood and my youth and my adult years. I have also traveled the paths of my faith trek: from Jackson Avenue United Methodist Church, to Divinity School, to various pastorates, to where I am now in service at Brentwood United Methodist Church. In my mind I have reread books, relistened to speeches, and revisited people who have had a strong influence on my life.

This spiritual pilgrimage has taught me several things. It has helped me to understand that I no longer need to prove anything to myself, to others, or to God. When we set out to prove ourselves, we usually wind up being a bit phony or defiant. When we honestly desire to be the unique person that God intended us to be, we are free to be more relaxed and in tune with what is going on in the lives of others.

I have also learned the value of being honest with how I feel. Leaders, be they political or religious, are often caught between what people want to hear and what people need to hear. If we put all of our energy into giving people what they want, the whole effort will go into calculating which way the wind is blowing. Jesus told his followers to merely say "Yes" or "No." By that, he meant for us to be gentle and nonjudgementally honest. To speak gently and without guile is important to me.

Another learning is the need that I feel to sharpen my powers of theological perception. The Church is not just another institution governed by normal organizational principles. It is a faith community under the Lordship of Christ, which seeks to provide for the maintenance of worship, the edification of believers, and the redemption of the world. I want to come to a deeper understanding of what God wants to do through the United Methodist Church. If I am to discern what God is "up to," I need to be more intentional with prayer, disciplined study, and the careful reflection. For me, this is a must because shallow, unfounded theology will not fit the complexities of today. To be more discerning seems to be an important task for pastoral leadership.

Taking a journey within myself has been both a painful and a joyful experience.

All in all, I have enjoyed meeting myself on the winding roadways of my inner map.

Why we want to know ourselves, and refuse to know ourselves, is worth pondering.

# For the Sake of Others

Since Pentecost Sunday, May 19, I have found myself doing a lot of introspection about my understanding of the Holy Spirit. Since that reflection is still with me, I want to use this column to think out loud about how I see the Holy Spirit.

Historically, the Holy Spirit has been seen as the third person of the Trinity. I believe that God shows himself in three ways—as Creator, as Redeemer, and as Holy Spirit. To say that God shows Himself as Holy Spirit is to say that God is "with us." Thus, God is not far removed and distant. Rather, God is near at hand and within us.

The Holy Spirit is not only with us, but it also does something. It empowers us to live out the Christian way of life. Without the empowering presence of the Holy Spirit, one is like a car without an engine. If we try to live without a dependence on the Holy Spirit, we will live only out of our own resources, and such living is not enough to get us through.

I also believe that there are certain evidences or signs of the Holy Spirit. The New Testament teaches that those who are open to the indwelling spirit of God bear certain fruit. The signs of the Spirit's presence are love, compassion, kindness, lowliness, meekness, patience, forbearance, forgiveness, and discernment—to mention but a few. Those who acknowledge and live by the Spirit are those whose lives manifest the fruits of the Spirit.

Unlike much of life, the Holy Spirit is not something that we work for in life. Working for something is one of the sure realities of life. We are meant to work for a living. Work at our relationships. Work at getting a good education. Work at outreach. Work at reconciliation. Work at achieving our goals. The Holy Spirit is not something that we work for in life. It is that which comes to us as a gift. It is God's gift that is freely given to all who wait with openness. Instead, the Holy Spirit is to be received like one receives the dawn and sunset of each day.

But, here is the catch. God does not give us the Holy Spirit for ourselves alone, and if we could possess the Holy Spirit for ourselves alone, we would not possess the Spirit at all. If we experience God as Holy Spirit, we experience Him not for ourselves alone, but also for others.

Above all else the Holy Spirit is given to the Church (us) for the sake of others.

It's worth pondering,

# Light and Warmth

L ast Friday evening Janene, Heather, Melanie, and I revived an old ritual. We went out to dinner as a family. When the girls were younger, those Friday night routines were almost habitual. We would go to dinner, then to a ball game, or to a movie, or shopping, or whatever.

But our daughters are now twenty-four and twenty-one years old respectively, and they now have their own way of keeping the sixth day of the week.

After placing our order we went to the salad bar. It was one of those that you walk around, and it had more stuff on it than any ten people could possibly sample. As I was piling on the lettuce, I noticed an older lady standing beside me. The top of her head came to my shoulder, and she was about as wide as she was tall. She was bedecked in well-maintained polyester. Underneath her pants legs I could see that she had on brand new canvas shoes. In five seconds I had enough clues to know that she was a tourist. So without blinking I said, "Where are you from?"

"Turkey Creek, Kansas," she said.

"Hope you have a wonderful time in Nashville," I replied.

"Oh, so do I. We took a tour today, Saw all of those big houses where the stars live. Could not believe what my eyes were telling me. Tonight, we are staying at the prettiest hotel anybody would ever want to see. And tomorrow night we are going to the Opry, and the next day we are going to drive all the way back to Kansas. Never thought I'd take a trip like this."

I noticed that she was not putting much on her plate. So I observed, "You must not be very hungry."

"Don't know if I am hungry or not. Think I am too excited to eat."

As we approached the end of the line I said, "Been nice talking to you, and I sure hope you have a great rest of the trip."

"Yes, sir, so do I, and I sure hope that I am not disappointed, because I have worked and saved and done without for a long time so that I could see these houses and hear these famous people sing, play, and tell jokes. Sure hope it is worth every penny."

This woman wanted to see and feel something that could not be experienced back in Turkey Creek, Kansas. She wanted to let more light and warmth into her life.

As Johann Wolfgang Goethe lay dying in 1832, one of his biographers reports that he sat up in bed and cried out longingly, "Light, light, more light!" This represented the central passion of his life, for he was easily the most learned person of his day, being the last of the so-called "universal men" who knew something about every field of human endeavor.

Years later, the Spanish philosopher, Miquel Unamuno, was reading this account and observed, "Goethe was mistaken. Instead of crying 'light, light, more light,' he should have called for warmth, warmth, more warmth." People do not die of the darkness; they die of the cold."

As I reflect on the human situation, people need both light and warmth in order to achieve a full humanity. Without light, we fall. Without warmth, we lose our affection for others. Both too little light and too little warmth can bring death.

Sunday is Pentecost Sunday. It's a time when we recount how the Holy Spirit was given to those first disciples, which resulted in the birth of the Christian Church. Then, as now, the abiding gift of the Holy Spirit brings both light and warmth.

I could not tell the lady at the salad bar that she would or would not be disappointed by the sights and sounds of Nashville. But I can tell you that you will not be disappointed if you are truly open to the Holy Spirit.

That this gift brings both warmth and light is worth pondering. How that happens will be the focus of Sunday's sermon.

# Good to be Wrong

There is something in me that wants to be right—being on target, being perceptive, being far-sighted is the way I would like to be. However, as much as I would like to be "on the money," I am often dead wrong.

I know that I should not own it in print, but I am more often wrong than I would like to admit. Most of the time I do not like to be off base. Hurts my inflated ego. Bumps my pride.

But I must admit that it is, at times, good to be wrong.

I was wrong about needing pews in the balcony. I honestly thought that we would not need the balcony, except for Christmas Eve and Easter, for another three to five years. Little did I knew that our worship attendance would move from a 1991 average of 1490, to an average of 1701 since moving into the new building. It was good to be wrong.

Prior to our having children, I thought that I would like to be the father of a girl and a boy. Had two wonderful daughters, and it was good to be wrong. I

202

was given an additional advantage in that both of the girls took after their mother!

When I was a student pastor, I thought that I wanted to go to the Decaturville Circuit. Much to my chagrin, I was sent to Enville. Had it worked out the other way I would have missed knowing Travis Canaday, one of the most unpretentious, down-to-earth, real people that I have ever had the pleasure of knowing.

Upon graduation from seminary I knew beyond any shadow of a doubt that I would spend my entire ministry in the Memphis Conference. Had it been "my way," I would have missed joining hands and hearts with the people of Brentwood United Methodist Church. I'm glad that I was wrong.

Thirty years ago I sincerely held to some beliefs that I no longer hold to be true. My mind has changed. I am now pleased to discover that I was wrong. (Someday I am going to do a series of "Ponderings" on how my mind has changed.)

Many of the people who experienced the life of Jesus were wrong in their assessment of him. They crucified him because he associated with the wrong people, taught the wrong things, and went the wrong places. A few—only twelve—were not wrong about Him. How fortunate for history that they were not wrong.

It takes a big person to say "I was wrong." Little people cannot say those three words. Little people get defensive, blame others, cover up, alibi, excuse themselves, or find some way to cop out.

When I was in the ninth grade, I wanted to make the Treadwell High School basketball team. I practiced, dreamed, planned, and did everything in my power to make the final cut. However, it was not to be. Since I did not make the squad, I had to take a sixth period class. The only one available was Miss Cooley's speech class. From there it was debate, acting, and competitive speech. Now, as I look back across these years, I am glad that I was wrong about basketball.

Life takes many funny turns. It is good that many of the turns are not of our own making. If it were left entirely up to us, we might unwittingly take the wrong path.

Often it is a grand relief to be wrong.

It's worth pondering.

# Love, Not Perfection

Today, there seems to be an undue preoccupation with personal growth and self fulfillment. There is nothing inherently wrong with seeking our own growth and development. I believe that God wants us to do that.

But there is something terribly wrong when we seek *only* our own growth and development. When the focus is totally on ourselves, trouble is just around the corner.

We need something to pull us out of ourselves, something to engage our hearts, something to activate our emotions, and something to help us experience God's presence in the human everydayness of life.

I, for one, need that which will balance my task-oriented temperament so that I can be involved at the deepest level with other people.

I need the kind of spirituality that will ground me in the real world so that I will never forget that love, not perfection, is where joy and the fulfillment of my soul is to be found.

It's worth pondering.

# Re-creation

St. Paul said that being in Christ is like putting on the new person and putting away the old. But there are many who want to put on the new life in Christ without putting away the old. We are reluctant to cast off the old being, although it is irreconcilable with the new life.

We want to believe, but not to obey; to rejoice, but not to amend our ways. We want to belong to God without putting an end to sin, to greed, to a lack of consideration, to haughty judgment, to the respectability and comfort of the old life.

Too many of us want to have our cake and eat it: God's love and self-love; God's mercy and our own merciless, self-centered hearts; God's joy and our sorrows. Multitudes want to live in God's Kingdom, without shouldering responsibility.

These things are mutually exclusive: to give one's heart to God and yet to remain as before; to receive God's love and yet be loveless. Reconciliation between these contradictory attitudes is impossible unless the old person is re-created by God.

When we allow ourselves to be recast, the old does not fit any longer.

It's worth pondering.

# Surrender Is Not a Dirty Word

Victory is our word. Not surrender. For many people, surrender is a negative term. It is like being given over to the authorities. Or, it is like waving a white flag. Or, it is like being defeated. Surrender is something that we are taught not to do. It should be shunned and avoided at all cost. Winning is the ultimate thing!

But in my opinion, surrender is something that all of us do. All of us, every single one of us, will surrender our lives to someone or something. At times we give our lives to that which is bad. On other occasions we contribute our souls to that which is good.

Most of the time we will surrender to something that we perceive as being bigger, more powerful, or more loving. Unconsciously, we allow ourselves to give in to that which promises to give us something in return.

So we surrender to work, to music, profession, families, ideas, concepts, perceived reality, mind-altering substances, relationships, or whatever. It is not something we knowingly choose. It is something that we do. Gradually, and over long periods of time, we drift into many forms of surrender.

I believe that we should be aware of that to which we surrender ourselves. Giving in to false gods can lead us to the underside of life. Surrendering to the God of Jesus Christ can bring the kind of joy that the world cannot give.

To what or to whom we are surrendering our soul is worth pondering.

# The Devil of the Noonday Sun

Things pop into my mind in strange ways and at odd times. Such happened last week when I was viewing the movie "Hoffa." It was in the midst of a violent scene, where union people were being clubbed, beaten, and thrown against brick walls with blood gushing six ways to Sunday. Without cause I thought, "What is the worst thing that can happen to a person?"

Possibilities started running through the maze of my mind. Death of a child? Death of a spouse or parent? Loss of a career or job? Being rejected? No education? Hunger? Moral failure? Being robbed or worse? Addiction? On and on the list went. All of these things hurt like whatever. But they are not the worst thing that can happen.

In my judgment the most difficult thing is what the old desert fathers called "acedia," which is tellingly described as "the devil of the noonday sun." Acedia is spiritual boredom or indifference to matters of faith. It leads to a heart so hard that it cannot feel for others. It can drag a person so far down that one is unable to live by his or her own principles. It leads to lack of feeling or caring. Not being alert to the transcendent, and only aware of the temporal, can so construct life that the life can go out of living.

For people who once had faith, acedia is not something that happens suddenly. Rather, it slips up on us, often unawares. It comes on slowly like the silent creeping of night into the otherwise brightness of day. It shatters the soul, leaving only the shell of a person.

One day Dr. Marney asked a class of young people studying for the ministry if they would still believe in Jesus Christ in ten years, or if they would be tamed by the local gentry. He was asking if their primary loyalties would shift.

We need to be on guard against the swing of our primary loyalties. When that happens, the death of the soul is not far behind.

It's worth pondering.

# Stewardship

# Consumer or Steward?

Recently, I have been reflecting on a persistent question—one of those nagging questions that will not go away. This inquiry has to do with how we will use this moment in history to really look at the future of the institutional church in general and the local congregation in particular.

In my opinion, this is not a time to merely tinker with structures, budgets, and forms with the hope that we can somehow make things right. Something deeper and more profound is needed. Something more far reaching is needed for the following reasons.

First, the culture no longer takes the Church as seriously as we take ourselves. How, in the words of St. Paul, are "we to be in the world but not of it"? If that is the case, what kind of Church do we need to be in order to carry out God's mission?

In the second place, many parishioners have a "consumerist" mentality. Like shoppers in a mall or grocery store, many churchgoers want to see some value for their money. Not a few have changed from being stewards into being consumers. There was a time when people united with a congregation because of beliefs or heritage. Now it seems that some persons join churches because of a youth program, or a music program, or a day school, or whatever. If the above assessment is true, how can we be the Body of Christ while addressing the "consumer mentality" that is in the Church?

Thirdly, there seems to be an increasing lack of commitment to anything beyond the needs and wants of the individual. R. Albert Mohler, editor of *The Christian Index,* says that we are living in a generation "that resists any sense of obligation." Responsibility and obligation are concepts that seem to be on the wane. My wife, Janene, hosts a dessert at our house every month for persons who have united with Brentwood United Methodist Church. We write a letter and include a response card. Our experience has been that about half of the people return the card, and about half of those who return the card actually attend. We have learned not to be upset about this, because it is characteristic of an age that does not feel a sense of obligation.

Fourthly, more time and energy are spent on maintaining institutional structures than on discerning what God is calling us to be. I know some leading denominational executives who took a retreat to study the management theories of a prominent thinker. Such study has its place in the Church, but it must not replace our going apart to discern God's will for the Church. Perhaps the Church leaders would have better served the Church if they had retreated to study Galatians or Acts. We must never forget that our marching orders come not from the gurus of business and technology, but from Scripture, theology, and the tradition of the Church.

Every congregation has the opportunity to be a symbol and to set the pace as an authentic expression of the Body of Christ.

It is both demanding and exciting to be part of a congregation that seeks to cut a new path and lift a high standard by calling its members to worship, teach, share, and heal.

How such values speak to a culture that no longer supports the Church is worth pondering.

# Free to Give

Mondays following Commitment Sundays are strange days for me. For thirty years I have experienced the Monday after. After going through thirty such Mondays, I still do not understand the feelings that swirl inside my skin. My thoughts range far and wide.

I think about those whose gift of time, talent, and money is a genuine and free expression of their faith! Supporting the continuing work of Christ on earth is a top priority with some people. Somewhere along life's path these people were freed for the joy of giving. Somewhere these people learned that joy, peace, and wholeness are to be found in the giving spirit.

Likewise, I reflect on those who are free to give only to themselves. Free to give themselves large wardrobes, spacious homes, the finest of food, up-to-date cars, nice trips, and plenty of entertainment. These are they who also give their children an over-abundance of material things, plus the finest of secondary and college educations.

Then, there are those who see the Body of Christ as just another organization in the community. No greater in its purpose than the "Y," the country club, the Boy Scouts, the political party, or the service club. For these, the Church holds no priority, nor does it make any special claim. It is just another organization with a different title.

I reflect on those who show no giving record, no time commitment, and no public worship, but who need the Church to be there for baptisms, weddings, funerals, hospitalizations, counseling, spiritual direction, and childcare. For these, being served by the Church is the primary agenda. Ironically, the Church at its best is there and will always be there, both for those who have given support, and for those who have not. When a call comes for a funeral, wedding, or hospitalization we never ask, "What have they done for the church?" But in the spirit of Christ, we pick up the towel and the washbasin as did our Lord. We are able to do this, because we believe that the Church lives to serve both those who are faithful and those who are not.

But the Monday after Commitment Sunday always drives me deep within myself. On this day I think not only about others, but also about myself. Thought pushes me to deeper reflection. Severe introspection fills most of the day. Such thought pushes me toward more fundamental questions.

The notion that has been pushing at me on this particular Monday is that we are all, to some extent, alike in our failure to be free, but some start out as being more handicapped than others. Not many of us are as free as we would like to be.

Most of us would like to be "freer" to be a giving people. But our freedom to give is hampered by the principalities and powers that hold us in bondage. Others of us are handicapped by our circumstances, parentage, background, selfishness, or because we do not truly believe that the message of Christ is the hope of the world.

Every year on the Monday following Commitment Sunday, I am reminded that in God's world there are givers and there are takers! Sometimes we are givers and at other times we are takers. Often we are a strange and conflicting mixture of both. In recent years I have learned that those who give enjoy a measure of freedom, which those who take never know nor understand.

And each and every year I am challenged and humbled by those who are free to give of themselves, that the work of Christ might continue in today's world.

Such was the case yesterday. I was moved, humbled, and overjoyed at such a generous outpouring.

Why some are free to share and why some are not is worth pondering.

# Serving and Keeping

When the famous Howard Hughes died at the age of 70, he was reputed to be "worth" more than two and a half billion dollars, and had become a complete recluse. *TIME* magazine wrote of him, "In his latter years Hughes had become the epitome of the 20th century tragedy, a man so preoccupied with gadgets and power that he severed the bond with his fellowmen." He had everything, but he had precious little.

At the other end of the spectrum are lives of ordinary people, who are provided a sense of worth and periodic dignity by the conventions, ceremonials, and the goals of the faith community to which they belong. I have known hundreds of people whose lives were so ordinary and inconspicuous as to seem to provide little more than props on the stage of life. Yet these prosaic souls could at least count upon the marriage of a daughter, or a trip to New York, or their own funeral to bring them some special prominence and even general esteem.

I have observed that the ordinary people seem to assume an everyday responsibility for the world and its affairs that one does not see in those who have severed the bond with other humans. Assuming responsibility for the world and not trying to master it should not be too narrowly associated with finances, because it involves caring for all that God has so graciously given.

Stewards are those who understand that all of creation is to be served and kept. Stewards are those who attempt to serve and keep:

- All that is in and of the world
- The building up of community
- The creatures of the earth

- Just and merciful political forms
- Channels for sharing

What motivates some to serve and keep, while others are driven to master and hoard?

It is worth pondering.

# Something for Which God Does Not Care

I sometimes fear that my mind runs in a counter-clockwise motion. It seems to contradict the prevailing notion of things as they are or as they appear to be. For example, a common view is that the happiest people are those who are always on the receiving end of things. Perhaps the opposite is true. Perhaps the happiest people are those who give the most.

Perhaps the reason that so many are so miserable is because they are not givers.

Marriages break up because people do not give to each other a full measure and running over. Children become separated from their parents because giving is absent in the relationship. The congregation that does not give to its community begins to die.

God wanted the children of Israel to be a light to the world. Instead, they kept the light for themselves and they moved steadily toward the loss of identity as the people of God. Jesus asked His followers to be the light of the world. But some people put the light under the bushel—which is just a way of saying that they kept it for themselves—and the light was extinguished. Life does not go well when we do not give to each other.

I have decided that God does not care whether or not we raise the church budget. But God does care passionately about our being givers. When we do not give, we are living contrary to the way God wired us up.

I believe that God wants us to find happiness, and the tried-and-true proven way to find happiness is by the pathway of giving.

As a pastor to thousands of people, I have discovered that the people who give their financial resources and themselves are the happiest people on earth. Those who hoard and keep always seem to be the most miserable.

It's worth pondering.

# The Tall One and the Short One

few weeks ago, Janene and I stopped at the Chattanooga Choo Choo for Sunday lunch. As we stood in line to purchase our lunch tickets, I noticed that the two women standing in front of us had something in common.

They were not the same size. One was tall and skinny as a rail. The other was short and fleshy. The tall one wore a solid blue suit with a red scarf draped around the shoulder. An oversized hat almost covered her distinctive facial features. Matching blue shoes complemented the outfit. The short one wore a buttoned-up red coat, which kept me from seeing the color of her dress. The coat had a tiny black collar and oversized gold button. A black pillbox hat was perched on her salt and pepper hair. Both women appeared to be "well fixed," as they say.

Though these two women were very different, they had one thing in common. They were both holding church bulletins. As they approached the cashier's window, they handed their bulletins to the lady behind the window. The cashier received the worship sheets, opened them, and ran her finger across the top of each page. After a careful scan, she put them aside and collected $7.95 from each customer. I thought it strange that a cashier would read and keep church bulletins.

But I put the thought away as Janene and I were being escorted to our table. After a few minutes we went to the buffet line for Sunday lunch. As I reached for a piece of fried chicken, I noticed that the tall and skinny lady was standing directly across from me. Since I enjoy probing strangers, I inquired, "I noticed that you gave away your church bulletin—is that what people do here in Chattanooga?"

With a big smile and great pride she said, "Well, not everybody does it, but I always do because of the fifty cents." "The fifty cents?" I replied with a questioning look etched on my face. "Yep," she squeaked with a high pitched, siren-type voice. "The half dollar goes to my church. I eat lunch here most every Sunday because this place is so generous to send fifty cents every week to our church budget. Wish more people would do their part. Sure would make things easier for the church. Why, if five hundred people would eat here every Sunday, we would get $250.00. Just makes sense to me. Besides, it's the way I pay my pledge."

As I walked back to the table, I thought that the restaurant owner would do handstands if five hundred people times $7.95 would follow the example of these two women (that's almost $4,000.00).

How some people will do almost anything to turn a profit, and how others will figure out ways to give without giving is worth considering.

As we drove out of the parking lot I waved to the tall one and the short one as they were climbing into their royal red Lincoln.

It's worth pondering.

# Worship

# Offering Ourselves

It is not unusual for me to hear people say something like, "Sometimes I do not get anything from church." I know what is meant by such statements, but there is another side to that coin. When we go to an athletic event, we are supposed to "get something out of it." When we read a book or go to the theater, we rightly expect to get some pleasure out of it. When we are involved in an educational endeavor, we should expect to gain knowledge. We approach many of life's experiences with the primary motive of gleaning something from them.

In my opinion, the primary—though not the only—reason for going to public worship is not what we can acquire from it, but what we can give to God through the experience. In corporate worship, what we give to God is more important than what we get.

Through worship we declare the "worthship" of God. In worship we *give* our attention to God through song, prayer, and the reading and hearing of God's Word. In the Service of Baptism we *give* our children over to the Church. At the Service of Death and Resurrection we *commend* our loved one over to God's eternal care. At the Service of Christian Marriage we *give* ourselves to each other and to the Christ who called us together at our baptism. At the Lord's Supper we *give* ourselves over to the Sacrament. Sunday morning worship is not getting. It is about giving God our adoration and praise.

If we come to the church expecting to get entertainment, or a spiritual massage, or goosebumps, we are setting ourselves up to be disappointed. When we come to worship focusing on what we can reverently give to Christ, we are opening ourselves up to that which is holy.

The reverse is also true. When we come to worship earnestly desiring to give to God, we find ourselves receiving more than we ever expected.

In public worship receiving always follows giving.

Why this is true is worth pondering.

# A World Shorn of God

Will we be formed by the living Christ, or will we be formed by the unseen intertwined forces of culture? The powers of culture are very strong. Money, sex, television, entertainment, malls, and the ethics of the street have the muscle to shape us. Their message is clear and convincing:

- Achievement and status are more important than what one believes
- The deepest needs of life will be satisfied if one worships the gods of sex, power, money, and sports
- The expression of emotion is more important than the control of emotion
- Self development is more important than self control
- Accepting guidance from anyone is a sign of weakness
- Power is to be determined not by service but by success
- Hope is to be found in the doctrine of more, and not in the power of love
- Winning is more important than the learning that comes from the defeats of life
- Peace and tranquility are more important than the strength that comes from struggle

I have decided that the forces that drive the unseen powers of culture do not care about us. They do not love us. They do not will the best for us. These "principalities and powers," as Paul called them, want to exploit us and hold us captive. They want us to serve them.

One day, Jesus told a story about a person who built a house upon a rock. When the rain fell and the wind blew, the house did not fall. He also told about another person who built a house upon the sand. When the storms of life came, the house did not stand.

If we do not build the house of our life on a solid foundation, our culture will shape us from a world shorn of God.

Why so many of us say that we believe in God, while worshiping the gods of our culture, is worth pondering.

# Getting Our Bearings

I like to attend church when I am on vacation. It's not because I am addicted to Sunday worship. It is that I, more than others, need the discipline of Sunday worship. In addition, I like to experience worship in different settings.

The two services that I attended were vastly different.

One service was folksy, showy, and self-congratulatory. It focused on those inside the chancel: the clergy, choir, liturgists, and the musicians. People came and went like they were in a movie house. In the midst of it all the sermon was excellent. The pastor was well prepared and reflective. His sermon was so good that I found myself thinking about it all week.

The other service was very reverent and "awe-filled." The congregation participated in every phase of the service. People sitting around me prayed the prayers, sang the hymns, and listened with care. In addition to a well prepared and beautifully delivered sermon, the service carried me toward the meaning of the text around which the service was built. Both dignity and warmth filled every square inch of the experience. Without a doubt, the people were participating in the "worship" of God.

At both services people were warm and responsive to me. Immediately following one service a man spoke to me, gave me his name, and invited me to lemonade and refreshments that were being served in a nearby hall. He asked, "Do you attend worship with regularity?" I said, "Yes, I go three times every Sunday morning forty-nine Sundays out of the year." His facial expression changed. Eyes got big like a bull frog. His hand, which was clasped in mine, started to sweat. With an uncertain sound he inquired, "Three different congregations or just one?" "Just one," I replied with some conviction in my voice. I thought that he would drop the subject.

Instead, he pushed on. "Do you hear three different sermons?" "Same one," I said. "Preacher must really be a good one," he replied. "Some days he's a lot better than others," I said. After a long pause, he caught on. And when he figured it out, he burst out with, "You must be clergy!" "Yes," I replied, "And I truly appreciated being in your worship service today. It was most inspiring."

Then the old man said, "Come every Sunday. Helps me get my bearings. Would not miss coming to worship for anything. Every Sunday, without fail, there is something that speaks to me. I've failed this church a lot of times, but this congregation has never failed me. Hope you will come and worship here again. Sure enjoyed sitting by you."

The other service had a "fellowship time" just prior to the sermon. Everyone was asked to stand and speak to each other. An older woman walked softly over to Janene and me and quietly said, "It's nice to have you here today." Her voice was genuine, warm, and receiving. With a few words and a caring expression she made us feel welcome. I knew that someone cared that we were present for the worship of God.

Each congregation worshipped God in a different way. Both churches were true to their understanding of how worship should be.

However, each congregation had something in common. They both knew how to welcome a stranger. In so-doing they followed the example of Jesus who recognized, received, and honored the stranger.

Why some people see the importance of welcoming the stranger, and why some do not, is worth pondering.

# The Bodily Glorification of God

Glorify God with your body. Glorify God with your body. Glorify God with your body. What did Saint Paul mean when he said, "Glorify God with your body"? I suppose St. Paul had a lot of time to think about things like that, because, after all, St. Paul spent a lot of time in jail. When you spend a lot of time in jail, you have some time to think about some things like glorifying God with your body.

This is hard for us to hear because we know how to glorify the body, but we do not know how to glorify God with the body.

I say to you that we know how to glorify the body. Recently, I bought one of these new little boxes that can be used to store things in closets. You can stack them, roll them, push them, and turn them upside down. When I put that little webbed box in my closet, I happened to look at all my clothing—trousers, shirts, suits, sport coats, and topcoats. Most of my clothing is there, not because I need it, but because I need to glorify my body.

A lot of the physical fitness craze today is not as much about physical fitness as it is about glorifying the body. Joggers pound the street and there is a plethora of work-out books. Why, you can even buy records and videos that tell you how to turn flab into firmness and fat into muscle. To be sure, it is important to stay in shape, but much of this craze is just to glorify the body.

But the Apostle Paul tried to correct that notion when he said, "Glorify God with the body. Glorify God with the body!"

How do we glorify God with the body?

We glorify God with the body when we physically do things that glorify God. Or, in other words, we glorify God with the body when we allow our bodies to be used in service to humankind. This is probably the greatest glorification of God with the body.

It is bodily involvement in Christianity that really matters.

The wonderful thing is that anybody can glorify God with the body. Chubby people, skinny people, distorted people, handicapped people, people like me who have to have a pair of trousers almost remade every time I buy them—any kind of body can glorify God. The culture in which we live says that only beautiful bodies are worth anything. Our faith says that everybody's body can glorify God.

It's worth pondering.

# What It Is!

Every now and then someone will do a magazine article on why people attend church. The article is usually based on some survey that has been conducted by a secular outfit of some sort. Most of the answers are usually as weak as water. "I want my children to learn Bible stores"; "I like the pastor—he preaches down-to-earth sermons"; "There is an early service and so we can still have most of the day to go bird watching";

"Our church is friendly and we need companionship"; "To become more established in the community"; "We love good music"; etc.

Rarely does anyone respond: "To worship God." Pure and simple. No frills. Straightforward. And yet that is the reason we come to church. Believers assemble to worship because God has called them together, whether they know it or not.

Worship is not entertainment. It is not a time when we come together to be the audience for actors on a stage. I have grown up on entertainment. Radio. Television. Theatre. Movies. Music. Personalities. Books. Newspapers. I enjoy the entertainment that is provided at almost every turn of my daily life. But that is not what Sunday worship is intended to be.

In worship, the community of God's people assemble to hear God's word spoken in Scripture, sermon, sacrament, music, and liturgy. Sometimes it is done well. At other times it is done poorly. But through it all something happens. That which is proclaimed and acted out in worship creates faith. And the faith which is created by that proclaimed word develops responses of praise, obedience, and commitment.

At no time has there ever been any kind of continuing life in relation to God apart from common worship. By participating year after year in corporate worship in which Scripture is central, God's people are prevented from creating a religion that's grown out of some private notion about God. They are also prevented from making a private, individualized salvation out of what they experience.

If at some time in the distant past, Christians had decided not to worship together, belief in Christ could not have been handed down from generation to generation. It is the discipline of common worship that enables the faith to be passed from person to person.

Every now and then I hear someone say, "I can worship God on the golf course, on the lake, and while walking by a mountain stream." I agree, because I have worshiped God in those places. But not on Sunday morning. If every Believer went his or her separate way, to do his or her own thing, where would the Word be read and proclaimed? The faith formed and handed down from one generation to another?

Being Christian is about being part of a community of those who trust the promises that God made in Christ.

It's worth pondering.

226

# Another Thought

One day, one of my students at Vanderbilt Divinity School asked, "What is the best church you ever served?" It was a difficult question to answer, but I said that Enville United Methodist Church would be near the top of the list.

I served Enville while I was a divinity school student from 1961–1964. The town of Enville is located in rural West Tennessee, not very far from the Tennessee River. The membership of the congregation was made up of farmers, homemakers, store owners, gin operators, and factory workers. About seventy five persons made up the membership of the congregation.

The Believers of Enville had a kind of wisdom that touched both the head and the heart. This wisdom came from living with a daily dependence on the land and each other. It is the clarity of thought that is stimulated by a loving and tight-knit community made up to about 300 souls.

In the early days of my ministry at Enville, my sermons sounded too much like my professors at the Divinity School. I was constantly weaving into my sermons that which I had heard my teachers say. In a word, I was far too cognitive in my preaching.

After one Sunday service, Faye Kent taught me a very important lesson. She gave me this advice while we were sitting around her dinner table. After we had finished our dessert, Faye said something like this, "Joe, when you are preparing sermons, think with your heart." It stuck. She did not need to say anymore. Even now I can hear her say, "think with your heart." Thank you, Faye.

To think with your heart does not diminish the need to do informed thinking, to think deeply, and to reflect theologically on the meaning of life. You see, when we let our heart interact with our mind we are better able to speak the truth in love; because when heart and mind are joined we are better able to understand what love requires.

It's worth pondering.